D0422373

RULES
OF
THUMB

RULES
OF
THUMB

ALAN M. WEBBER

52

TRUTHS FOR
WINNING AT BUSINESS
WITHOUT LOSING
YOUR SELF

HARPER
BUSINESS

An Imprint of HarperCollins*Publishers*
www.harpercollins.com

RULES OF THUMB. Copyright © 2009 by Alan M. Webber. All rights reserved. Printed in the United States of America. No part of this book may be used or reproduced in any manner whatsoever without written permission except in the case of brief quotations embodied in critical articles and reviews. For information, address Harper-Collins Publishers, 10 East 53rd Street, New York, NY 10022.

HarperCollins books may be purchased for educational, business, or sales promotional use. For information, please write: Special Markets Department, HarperCollins Publishers, 10 East 53rd Street, New York, NY 10022.

FIRST EDITION

Library of Congress Cataloging-in-Publication Data is available upon request.

ISBN 978-0-06-172183-0

09 10 11 12 13 OV/RRD 10 9 8 7 6 5 4 3 2 1

To my mother and father and my brother, Mark
To Frances, Adam, and Amanda

To Cobie, Timmie, and Iko

To my aunts and uncles, cousins, nieces, and nephews

To all the remarkable people I worked for, worked with,
and learned from, whether named or unnamed in this book,
all of whom I deeply appreciate

To my mother and father and my brother, Mark
To Frances, Adam, and Amanda

To Cobie, Timmie, and Iko

To my aunts and uncles, cousins, nieces, and nephews

To all the remarkable people I worked for, worked with,
and learned from, whether named or unnamed in this book,
all of whom I deeply appreciate

WHO KNOWS THE RULES?

These are extraordinary times.

In our work, our lives, and everything in between we are witnessing change that is so fast and unpredictable that our first challenge is simply to make sense of it.

Globalization, technology, and the knowledge economy have propelled countries, industries, companies, and individual careers into new and uncharted territory. Unprecedented and destabilizing economic, political, and social events are unfolding. Massive financial shifts have undermined the leading economies of the world. Old, prestigious companies with long, storied heritages have disappeared overnight. Entire industries have awakened to discover that they need to adapt, transform, or become extinct. It's no exaggeration to say that leading thinkers around the world are seriously discussing new forms and new rules for the future of capitalism.

At the same time, because economic creation always accompanies economic destruction, a new generation of entrepreneurs is seizing the moment. As giant companies appeal to Washington, D.C., for financial aid, brand-new start-ups suddenly emerge to capture the public's imagination—and the market's wallet. Financial and business fissures have opened to innovation, invention, and inspiration.

The time has come to rethink, reimagine, and recalibrate what is possible, what is desirable, what is sustainable.

It's time to rewrite the rules.

We're badly in need of rules of thumb that work, that make sense, that can guide us through and past these turbulent times. Rules of thumb that teach us how to work—and also inspire us to understand why we work. Rules of thumb that show us higher roads to take in our business and personal lives—and demonstrate that those two roads are best traveled as one. Rules of thumb that suggest a code of conduct for each of us as individuals and for all of us as a community. We want rules of thumb that help us succeed—and help us win at work without losing the people and things we care most about in life.

That's what *Rules of Thumb* is about. It's a collection of fifty-two rules I've gathered over the last forty years or so. During that time I've met and worked with a series of remarkable men and women who have given me their wisdom and helped me make sense of my own experiences. I've talked with famous leaders who are world-renowned and learned from obscure entrepreneurs who are unknown; I've sat with brilliant Nobel Prize winners whose scientific discoveries cure millions and visited modest community organizers who change the world one person at a time—and learned valuable lessons from all of them. I've interviewed CEOs and spiritual leaders, basketball coaches and novelists, business thinkers and elected officials—and come away with fresh insights and hard-won truths.

I've recorded those lessons on three-by-five cards that I carry with me every day at home and on the road. (This wonderful system is something I learned more than twenty years ago from Harvard Business School professor Ted Levitt, one of the mentors you'll meet in this book.)

Not long ago, I reviewed all the three-by-five cards I'd written on and saved. This time my goal was to capture the rules I'd learned. I began to fill up three-by-five cards until I reached fifty-two, at which point I stopped. Not because I'd run out of rules, but because they represented the best of what I'd learned and what I had to pass on.

Because I want you to understand where these rules came from, each has a story about how I learned it. In almost every case they come from four deep experiences I've had in my life:

- In the early 1970s, after graduating from Amherst College, I went to Portland, Oregon, where I worked for Mayor Neil Goldschmidt, and with the committed, forward-thinking team he put together in city hall, as well as the community of activists across the city who transformed Portland into the urban showcase it is today. It was an education in urban planning, electoral politics, and the art of making change.

- In the 1980s I worked for Ted Levitt and with the creative, dynamic group he assembled at the *Harvard Business Review* (*HBR*) to reinvent that prestigious journal and to change the business conversation at the highest level. I was the beneficiary of a free education in business and management and in the art of combining best thinking with best practice.

· In the 1990s I partnered with Bill Taylor and a hard-charging, fast-thinking, and marvelously adventuresome team to launch and edit *Fast Company* magazine, the fastest-growing business magazine in U.S. history. It was an education in entrepreneurship and in leadership; it was the hardest and most rewarding thing I'd ever done.

· In the 2000s, since leaving *Fast Company*, I've explored new ideas, new directions, and new experiences—serving as an advisor to the KaosPilots, a Scandinavian school for social entrepreneurs, and as chairman of the Waldzell gathering, an Austrian conference that takes place at the historic Abbey of Melk. As a self-appointed minister without portfolio, a self-styled global detective, I've traveled, consulted, and entered a new world of teachers and a wide variety of experiences.

But this book isn't about me; it's *for* you.

The whole purpose of *Rules of Thumb* is to stimulate, inspire, challenge, and help you. Read it, use it, apply it in any way that works for you. It's a book of rules—but there is no rule about how to read it.

You can start at Rule #1 and work your way to Rule #52.

You can use it as an I Ching for work and life: open it to

wherever the pages happen to fall, and consider that rule your day's reading.

You can read one rule per week and make reading *Rules of Thumb* a year of self-discovery.

Read the ones that make sense to you; skip the ones that don't—for now, at least. You can always check back later and see if something in your life or in the world has changed to make what seemed obscure or irrelevant suddenly make sense. Make your own notes about the rules that speak to you. Talk back to the book, talk back to the rules.

Most important, start keeping your own three-by-five cards to capture your own rules. You'll find that you'll pay closer attention to your own experiences; you'll collect your own network of teachers; you'll discover ideas that matter to you and help you make sense of the world.

You'll start having a conversation with your own life and your own experiences. Those three-by-five cards will stack up as you take note of the best conversations you get into— including the ones with yourself. You'll discover rules of thumb in your daily life that work for you.

That's what Rule #53 at the end of the book is for. I left that one open. Send your contribution to www.rulesofthumb book.com or e-mail alan@rulesofthumbbook.com. I'll collect them and post them so we can learn from each other.

More than anything, here's what this book is about:

It's about what works.

It's about a way of learning what works and applying it to your own life.

It's about the value of experience and observation—of life lived and life reflected on.

It's about what all of us can learn from our own experience and from each other.

It's about change—and how to make sense of change.

And it's about what doesn't change, the fundamentals of life well lived and work well done.

Each of us—and all of us—are in charge of generating our own rules of thumb to guide us through times of great turbulence, uncertainty, and opportunity. We need to be our own best thinkers and best doers, best teachers and best learners.

We may be on different journeys, but we're on different journeys together. Each of us can generate our own rules of thumb; all of us can learn from each other. It's our best hope for creating the future we all want.

RULES
OF
THUMB

WHEN THE GOING GETS TOUGH, THE TOUGH RELAX.

The year was 1986. I was sitting at the end of a formal boardroom table in a private office in the German Bundestag in Bonn. I had on my best three-piece suit and a Brooks Brothers tie I'd bought for the occasion.

I was waiting to conduct an interview with former German chancellor Helmut Schmidt for the *Harvard Business Review*. I'd written my questions out in longhand on a yellow legal pad. My tape recorder was plugged in and strategically placed on the table near the chair where I assumed Chancellor Schmidt would sit. I'd calculated the angle of the recorder so I could make eye contact with Schmidt and check the machine. The last thing I needed was to sit through the interview only to discover afterward that the recorder had malfunctioned. I was jet-lagging like crazy, having flown from Boston to Bonn the night before. And I couldn't stop going over in my mind all the ways this interview could go wrong—and everything that was riding on it.

At that moment right before Helmut Schmidt walked into the room I realized I was going about this in a way that was guaranteed to blow it.

My approach was wrong.

My mind-set was wrong.

And if I didn't do something to change it in the next few seconds, I'd not only doom my project but also feel bad about it for the rest of my life.

The problem was how I'd gotten to that room in the first place.

A short time before this trip to Germany, the brilliant, curmudgeonly marketing guru Ted Levitt had taken over as faculty editor of the *Harvard Business Review*. I was working there as an associate editor, at the bottom of the pecking order. And I was bored out of my mind by the publication's stuffy complacency.

It turned out that Ted shared my evaluation of *HBR*. He characterized it as "the only magazine written by people who can't write for people who don't read." As soon as he took over as faculty editor, overseeing the staff of professionals, Ted set out to shake the place up. At the top of his to-do list was to hold an internal competition for a new managing editor, the title that went to the highest-ranking staff member. When Ted interviewed me about my intentions for the future, much to my own surprise the words that came out of my mouth were, "I either want to run this place or leave it."

To make my bid for the top job I'd proposed a series of interviews: "The Statesman as CEO." I would travel around the world and interview former heads of state to explore leadership—but of a country, not a company. I'd start with Helmut Schmidt, then interview Japan's Yasuhiro Nakasone, the United Kingdom's James Callaghan, and finally former U.S. presidents Gerald Ford and Jimmy Carter.

There was a method to my madness. Years before, the German Marshall Fund had selected me for a fellowship, a three-month stint in Munich to study that city's urban plan. I figured that by working through the German Marshall Fund, I could line up an interview with Helmut Schmidt. Once I had one statesman committed I could use him as leverage with the others. Sure enough, when I called my contact at the German Marshall Fund, she told me that an interview would indeed be doable. But she also warned me that I might not enjoy the experience.

"He's not a very pleasant man," she advised me. "He's very hard to interview because he looks down on the people asking the questions. And," she confided, "you know he takes snuff."

Nevertheless, she had me send a formal proposal on official *HBR* stationery that she could forward to the appropriate German authorities. After my request went through the proper channels my friend came back with a date, a time, and a place for my interview with the notoriously difficult, snuff-taking chancellor.

All that was going through my mind as I sat there staring at my tape recorder and my yellow lined legal tablet.

What would Ted Levitt think if I screwed up this interview?

What would happen to my chances for the top job at *HBR*?

More immediately, what would happen if Helmut Schmidt dismissed my questions as stupid?

What if the tape recorder malfunctioned?

I looked at it sitting there, waiting for the opportunity to betray me. I could feel the pressure rising in my chest.

That's when I took my pen out of my shirt pocket and carefully wrote new instructions to myself. I put them at the top of the yellow legal tablet above all my questions, where my eyes would come to rest before I started the interview and between every question: "Relax! Smile! This is a blessing, a treat, and an honor. It's not a punishment to be endured."

How many people get to sit across from a world leader and ask him questions? How many people get to see their proposal for a project—any project—approved, and then get to go do it?

What I needed to see was how fortunate I was to be there. To enjoy it. To relax and hope that Helmut Schmidt would enjoy it. To see it as it really was: an exceptional experience.

I had just written the instructions to myself at the top of the tablet when the door opened. Chancellor Schmidt walked in.

We shook hands. I introduced myself and briefly explained the project. I got ready to ask my first question. But first I smiled. He smiled back.

So What?

W. Edwards Deming is famous for his fourteen-point program that created the modern total quality movement. The one I always come back to is his eighth point: "Drive out fear, so that everyone may work effectively for the company."

What he didn't say is that the place to start is with you.

Anytime you approach a task with fear you are at least a double loser. First, you color the work with fear and increase the chances of failure. Confidence and composure trump fear every time. Second, you guarantee that you won't enjoy the experience. Whether you succeed or fail, wouldn't you like to remember the experience as one you enjoyed, not one you suffered through?

So when you feel that familiar unpleasant sensation rising up in your chest or settling into the pit of your stomach, remember Rule #1. Don't let fear undermine your chance to do that one thing you've wanted to do. Rule #1 touches every other rule. Take a second and smile. Enjoy the trip.

EVERY COMPANY IS RUNNING FOR OFFICE. TO WIN, GIVE THE VOTERS WHAT THEY WANT.

Back in 1999 I was invited to a special appearance by then-senator Bill Bradley, who was running for the Democratic nomination for president. The event was held in the penthouse at the Kennedy School of Government, and I went because I admired Bradley as an elected official and a basketball player—and a fellow Missourian.

After the usual pleasantries Bradley began his informal talk by describing the terms the Kennedy School had set as preconditions for his appearance.

Bradley said, "When they called me they said, 'We're a patriotic institution, so we have to ask you some questions. Do you support the Constitution of the United States?' I told them I did. They said, 'Do you support freedom of religion?' Yes, I said. They said, 'Freedom of assembly?' Yes, I said, I support freedom of assembly. They said, 'Free speech?' Yes, I said. 'Good,' they said, 'because you're going to give one.'"

Bradley's opening joke may accurately reflect the political values at the heart of America; more importantly, it serves as a reminder that business and politics have to meet the same test—the American character test. Whether you know it or not, your company is running for office. You're a campaign manager, trying every day to win the votes of the American consumer. And as in any campaign, knowing the answer to the question, "What do those voters want?" dramatically increases your chances of winning.

So what *do* American voters want?

I'd start with the most fundamental of all qualities: Americans are uniquely practical. We want things that work. For the most part we leave it to others to argue over philosophy, metaphysics, abstractions. We Americans pride ourselves on our ability to get things done. We do what it takes to make things happen, and we want products and services that do the same.

The second fundamental American attribute is adaptability. Among all the nations in the world we are unique in our steadfast belief that everything, including ourselves, can be made better. We're the folks who invented the notion that "every day in every way I'm getting better and better." We invented an entire industry around the theme of self-improvement. In the United States the idea that we can all get better, get smarter, and get ahead is hardwired into our national consciousness. Any idea that can be launched in version 1.0 is quickly in line for a new, improved, upgraded version 2.0. Everything can be made to work even better.

Third, we Americans have always been obsessed with innovation. What's new, what's next, what's never been done before—these are intrinsically American concerns. Today innovation has practically become an American cliché, the path to the future for companies in every industry. But companies and their leaders aren't wrong to make this claim. It's as American as you can be, going back to one of our nation's founding innovators, Benjamin Franklin.

What do voters want from our companies?

We want things that work. We want to be able to make them work better. And we want to find things that both work better and are innovative. Three qualities that aren't mutually exclusive. They're mutually reinforcing.

Have you got what the voters want?

So What?

You're in business. Every day you're running for office. Every vote counts. Every day you have to prove to your customers that you're worthy of their votes. You have to show them that you get them. That you care about them. That you care about the same things they care about.

What do they care about?

· Does it work?

· Can we make it work better?

· Is it new and better?

Measure your business ideas and performance against this deeply American scorecard. If what you have to offer stacks up well, you've got a head start at winning the hearts and minds—and wallets—of the American market.

For the first issue of *Fast Company*, Mark Fuller, the co-founder and CEO of Monitor Company, wrote a provocative essay called "Business as War."

The third section of the piece, called "Why Companies Fail, Part 2," taught me a lesson I've carried with me since the first time I read it. Here's what it says: "Right through the Vietnam War, big companies and the military shared the same approach to strategy. Both labored under institutional dynamics that virtually guaranteed competitive defeat. The terrible irony of Vietnam was that the United States won every battle but lost the war. Most military histories of the Vietnam War agree on the reason for the defeat: the military had no unified strategic doctrine, no clear definition of victory."

No clear definition of victory. That's the lesson.

If you have no clear definition of victory, how do you know when—or if—you've won? For that matter, how do you know why you're fighting in the first place?

If you have no clear definition of victory, how do you allocate your resources? How do you deploy your people? How long do you stick with it, and how do you know when you've reached your goal?

I began to take this message to heart with our own fledgling magazine: What was our definition of victory? How would we know with each issue and with the magazine as a whole whether we were winning or losing?

Bill Taylor, my partner in launching *Fast Company*, and I decided that we didn't want to be the biggest magazine with the largest circulation. We did want to be profitable, but our goal wasn't to make the most money of any magazine.

No, our definition of victory would be *impact*. We wanted our readers to find articles that were so useful, so valuable—so impactful—they'd clip them and save them or send them to a friend. We wanted to be the first word—but not the last—in a dialog with our readers about the future of business. An issue would be a victory if we published at least one article that moved the needle when it came to our readers' responses. We kept track of the e-mails we got from readers; we noted which articles stimulated the most feedback. The best e-mails would say, one way or another, "How did you know what I was thinking?" That's when we knew we'd scored on impact.

After a while "definition of victory" began to sound a little too militaristic. No surprise there, since Mark's essay was titled "Business as War." I felt more comfortable asking, "What's the point of the exercise?" In other words, what are we trying to achieve? Why are we doing this in the first place?

Most of the time, I discovered, whether it was something we were considering doing at *Fast Company* or it was an idea a friend was proposing, the real answer was "I don't really know." Or "I kind of know—but not really."

Now, the point of asking "What's the point of the exercise?" isn't to humiliate anyone. It's simply the most clarifying question you can ask. It's the best thing you can do for yourself or anyone asking your advice. Because if you don't know what the point of the exercise is, honestly, accurately, and crisply, then you're going to wander around a lot, wasting your time and energy on something you don't really understand.

When you can answer the question "What's the point of the exercise?" and do it from your head and your heart, then you're ready to launch your project. And ready to succeed at it.

So What?

To me this is the litmus test.

Do you know the point of the exercise?

This simple question is actually a way for you to reverse-engineer your project: Until you ask the last question about what you're going to do you can't really get started. So ask the last question first and then work your way back from that to the beginning.

Here's another hint based on my own experience: Whatever your first answer to that question, it's usually not the right one. Keep asking the question—of yourself, of your friends when they come for advice, of your business partners and associates. It usually takes at least three times before you get to an honest answer. And dishonest answers don't help.

Do we really know why we're doing this?

You might answer, "To make a lot of money."

Or "To make a big difference."

11

You might even answer, "Both!"

Don't do that. That's another trap. Don't cheat and simply say, "All of the above." The point of asking the question is to put yourself on the hook. Sure, it's uncomfortable—that's the point. Wriggling off the hook feels better, but it's too easy. It avoids giving a hard answer to a hard question.

But if you don't work for that hard answer, if you avoid having to confront why you're doing something, you won't know the right way to do it or even whether you should do it in the first place.

"What's the point of the exercise?" is the kind of question that will keep you honest. It's the right place to begin any new adventure. At the other end of the road it will help you know when you've arrived at your self-determined destination.

DON'T IMPLEMENT SOLUTIONS. PREVENT PROBLEMS.

We're all interested in real solutions that work.

In business, tough-minded leaders focus on results. To underscore the point, business thought leaders such as Larry Bossidy, A. G. Lafley, and Ram Charan have scored big hits with books teaching executives how to focus on execution. Putting solutions into effect seems to be where the action is.

But what if the real action isn't with solutions? Focusing on solutions misses an essential point: preventing problems in the first place. There's an even more important idea than execution. It's the idea of early detection, intervention, and prevention. Business leaders who embrace that idea can point at something even better than implementation. They can point at massive savings and better outcomes.

I learned this lesson thanks to one of the most inspiring leaders I've ever met, Pittsburgh's Bill Strickland. Ten years ago I met Bill over the kitchen table of my next-door neighbor's house in Brookline, Massachusetts. That night, after

Bill told his story, I knew two things: Bill was going to change things in America, and Bill and I would be friends for life.

Here's the way Bill explained the choice we all have to make.

It's no secret that we put a lot of young people in jail in America. In fact, the United States is the world's most imprisoned country. (That's right: we're number one in prison population.) Today more than 2.2 million Americans are behind bars, more than one in a hundred American adults. Roughly one in eight black men between the ages of twenty-five and twenty-nine is incarcerated. In Bill's home state of Pennsylvania the prison population is more than forty-five thousand, having grown every year since 1976.

Assume that you look at this problem as if it were strictly business. You want to know the cost to taxpayers to keep these young men behind bars. And you want to know if it's working.

Last year the taxpayers of Pennsylvania spent $1.6 billion on corrections. And because the number of inmates keeps rising, the head of corrections asked taxpayers for another $600 million to build new prisons. For that money the good people of Pennsylvania get . . . well, it's hard to say exactly what they get. Probably they get a more hardened criminal who comes out of jail worse off than he went in. They get an embittered young black man with a criminal record and no skills who can't get a job and has few prospects for the future. They get a recidivism rate approaching 50 percent, which means that one-half of all inmates return to prison within three years of their release. On the other hand, they can be proud that the Commonwealth of Pennsylvania is hard at work executing a solution to the problem of crime. That's implementation for you.

Compare that approach to Bill Strickland's program at the Manchester Craftsmen's Guild in Pittsburgh. For the last forty years, Bill, who happens to be African American and a recipient of the MacArthur Foundation "genius" award, has been offering his students real educational opportunity, real marketable skills, real self-respect, and a real future. Bill is in the hope business, and his customers are young men and women, black and white, who might otherwise end up in serious trouble.

There are no metal detectors at Bill's school, no police to keep order. But there is a culinary arts program that trains young people for jobs in the best kitchens in America—and also serves up world-class meals to the other students.

There's no graffiti on the walls—but there are paintings, photos, and works of art on display, all created by the students.

There's even a gorgeous music hall for concerts. It's such a great facility that nearly all of the famous black jazz musicians in America have performed there. Bill's team has recorded those performances and released a set of CDs, with the proceeds coming back to help finance the school. But it's not just money that comes back—it's also recognition. Bill may run the only antipoverty, anticrime educational program in the world that has also won four Grammy awards.

The cost per pupil at Bill's program is $1,500 per year. And it has an 85 percent college placement rate for graduating seniors.

But the key to Bill's school isn't the cost. The key is where he intervenes in the lives of the young people. It's all about early detection and early intervention, rather than incarceration or remediation. Bill's program delivers prevention—and, as the old saying goes, an ounce of prevention is worth a pound of cure.

So What?

Bill Strickland's program happens to be a nonprofit that delivers education, training, and hope.

But the rule he practices applies to every business.

It's the fundamental principle behind the rise of the total quality movement in the United States—but only after the Japanese systematically ate this country's lunch in one manufacturing industry after another. U.S. companies were trying to inspect quality at the end of the assembly line. They could have executed like crazy with all those inspections, catching defect after defect. They still would have lost to the Japanese, who were preventing defects from happening in the first place.

Why were business leaders able to see this principle in the one area of total quality but were unable to apply it in other areas? (For that matter, why haven't we been able to apply it in a host of public policy areas? We know that prevention and early intervention work in everything from health care to energy policy to public education to transportation. But these well-entrenched systems seem intractable, despite economic and social evidence that proves how much more effective and less expensive a different approach would be.)

Companies still don't apply early intervention and prevention in something as basic as customer service. After a company has thoroughly alienated its customers with poor service, lousy attention, and insulting marketing pitches, it then tries to make it up with insincere apologies.

At the top of major corporations leaders habitually look the other way when they know a serious problem needs their attention, hoping the day of reckoning won't come on their watch. Or they pound the table and demand a fix—without ever acknowledging that their inattention to the root cause of the problem only drives up the cost of any solution, which is often not a solution but only a palliative.

You could chalk it up to human nature: denial, hope against hope that somehow the inevitable won't happen, at least not yet.

But there is another component to human nature, and all it takes is practice: look reality in the eye, establish an honest assessment of the real nature of the problem, look upstream to see its true causes, and then roll up your sleeves and attack it early, deeply, and effectively.

In the end it's not only cheaper and more effective. It also represents leadership and a very valuable skill. It's the kind of talent that wins MacArthur prizes.

Just ask Bill Strickland.

CHANGE IS A MATH FORMULA.

Here's the formula. Change happens when the cost of the status quo is greater than the risk of change: $C(SQ)>R(C)$.

I learned this formula in the fall of 1970, having just graduated from Amherst College. With a bunch of my things piled in the back seat of my blue Mustang, I drove across America and arrived in Portland, Oregon.

On a typical gray Portland day I crossed the Steel Bridge, found a parking spot downtown, got out of the car, and thought, "I don't know exactly where I've arrived, but here I am."

One of the things I didn't know then and only found out about a year later was that I'd arrived in Portland at a moment when the city's future was hanging in the balance. Another thing I didn't know was that I'd spend the next decade working with a brilliant young mayor, a committed staff, and a dedicated community to build a future for Portland that would make it the most livable, forward-looking city in the United States.

But that's not how Portland looked in 1970.

Back then Portland was a backwater—and proud of it. Let San Francisco enjoy its smug sophistication and Seattle its Boeing-based boom. Portland in 1970 looked more like a city trapped in the 1950s. Dragging the gut—driving a hot car up and down the Broadway couplet in the heart of downtown—was still the coolest thing to do on a Friday night. Having been built on the timber industry, Portland came across as a roughneck town, with a skid row filled with homeless drunks and run-down flophouses. There was a small high-rise office core, but most of the office buildings downtown were old and tired. The city's power structure matched downtown's appearance: in 1970 the mayor and city council averaged more than seventy years of age.

That much was apparent even to a newcomer like me.

What wasn't so obvious was the map to the future the city elders had drawn, most importantly the comprehensive freeway map that was the city's official transportation plan. Shortly after the end of World War II Portland had hired New York's master builder, Robert Moses, to design a new transportation vision. Moses gave Portland what he'd already given New York: a massive sprawl of freeways slicing through the city's residential neighborhoods. In fact, if all the freeways Moses called for had been built, one out of ten houses in the city of Portland would have been bulldozed to build a freeway or would have ended up next to a freeway.

It was a transportation vision that would have made Portland into a mini Los Angeles. The city's neighborhoods would have been sacrificed to the cars moving through them. Families would have been displaced to the suburbs.

Urban sprawl would have reshaped the region. And Portland would have been left as the hole in the middle of the regional doughnut, a city of the poor, the old, and the very young, people who couldn't afford to move to the suburbs.

That was the status quo. That was the road map to the future the city was using, until a charismatic young former Legal Aid attorney named Neil Goldschmidt changed the math.

Neil was a real Oregonian. Raised in Eugene, he'd attended the University of Oregon, where he'd been elected student body president. He'd gone to law school at Berkeley and worked in Mississippi during Freedom Summer as part of the civil rights movement. Back in Portland he'd worked for Legal Aid and then, at the age of twenty-seven, run for city council, an injection of youth into a geriatric body.

As a candidate he objected to the way the council did its business—behind closed doors in private meetings before the make-believe public sessions. He objected to the way city planning ignored the needs of Portland's neighborhoods. Most of all, he objected to the Mt. Hood Freeway, the first leg of Moses' grand transportation plan that was getting ready to move ahead.

When he won his election he asked the mayor to give him city planning as his portfolio. The mayor handed him the animal control bureau to manage. The next year Neil announced his candidacy for mayor.

When he opened his campaign Neil's brochure carried a quote on the cover from his announcement speech: "Ours is a city with much to cherish, much to love, and too much to lose to remain idle." The campaign itself was a math lesson.

What is the cost of the status quo?

What is the risk of change?

The cost of the status quo, beginning with the Mt. Hood Freeway, turned out to be exorbitantly high: bulldozing neighborhoods, adding air pollution, dumping more cars into the already auto-clogged downtown—all to build a freeway that the environmental impact statement showed would be filled bumper to bumper the day it opened. The price tag was the destruction of everything the people of Portland loved about their city.

The risk of change—well, that was embodied by Neil Goldschmidt.

He talked very fast—his political opponents mocked his speaking style as "rat-a-tat-tat." He was a young man in a hurry, and that in itself was risky. In some parts of Portland he was whispered against because he was Jewish.

Political campaigns are, in part, a chance for voters to do the math. In the end the people of Portland decided that the cost of the status quo was higher than the risk of change. When the votes were counted on election day, Portlanders had elected Neil as their new mayor, the youngest big-city mayor in the United States.

If you go to Portland today, take a look at the light rail lines that were built instead of the freeways. Stay in the vibrant downtown and visit the healthy neighborhoods. You can see that Portlanders got the math problem right. The cost of doing nothing would have been much higher than the risk of change.

So What?

I learned this lesson more than thirty years ago. Since then I've been involved in and written about dozens of change efforts, some in government, some in companies. Usually they involve deeply committed people who believe in their cause, are convinced they're right, and are prepared to sacrifice their careers, if that's what it takes to win.

Most of the time they lose and sacrifice their careers.

It doesn't have to be that way. But most of the time it is. Why?

Because it's not enough to be convinced that you're right. The other side is equally convinced that it's right. If you're a change agent inside a company and you're campaigning for the CEO to pick your side because you're "right," most of the time you're going to lose. If you turn change into an "it's him or me" decision, and you've announced that you'll stake your career on the choice, you can start packing your personal effects. You'll end up sounding like a militant zealot—which is another way of saying martyr.

On the other hand, if you actually want to win, rather than settling for dying for your cause, there are some techniques and tactics you can learn that will change the math in your favor.

First, you've got to be clear in your own thinking that you're in the game for the long haul, not staking your career on a quick victory. It doesn't matter if you're trying to get your company to adopt a new strategy, if you want the marketing department to make a fundamental change in its approach, or if you want a new recruiting and hiring policy to bring new talent into the company—whatever the cause, if you care enough to fight, you've got to care enough to stay and fight. When it comes to making change, Yogi Berra was only half right: it's never over till it's over—and it's still not over then. The same battles keep reoccurring in companies and in politics, and you've got to be there to fight them with your eyes on the long-term outcome.

Second, you've got to learn the other side's language and know its arguments better than it does. When we were trying to change Portland's transportation future, we needed more than just the environmental arguments. We had to be able to speak traffic engineer. We had to prove that the freeway was not only bad for neighborhoods and air quality, but also a bad way to move cars. The argument that the freeway would be filled to capacity the day it opened was a traffic argument the other side couldn't refute.

In general, it's a good idea to learn to speak economics, if you can't already. That's because people on both sides of a fight respect the dollars and cents of an issue. Proving that your solution is less expensive and works better makes your moral arguments all the more compelling.

Third, it's not enough to be against something that's bad—you've got to be for something that's better. This is especially true if you're trying to convince the boss—or the voters—that the status quo isn't good for them. Political pros know that something always beats nothing. If all you're offering is nothing, the old something, bad as it is, will win. Frustrated as you may be by the status quo, keep your powder dry until you've worked out the details, the arguments, the economics, and the math of your much better alternative.

Finally, look for allies. Too often change agents paint

themselves into a corner with their arguments—and find themselves all alone when they get there. But a genuinely creative change effort will cut across traditional boundaries and disrupt old alliances. If you do your math right and you figure out how to allocate the true costs of the status quo while driving down the risks of change, you may discover some new allies you can bring to your side—people you might ordinarily write off as "conservative" or "risk-averse." Woo them to your cause. Convince them that your solution is as conservative as they are—because it saves money, it's more efficient, it has fewer unintended consequences, change is actually the lower-risk road to take, and it actually works.

Learning to make change is all about learning to do the math of change. Done right, it's not just a soft art, it's also a hard science.

IF YOU WANT TO SEE WITH FRESH EYES, REFRAME THE PICTURE.

Ted Levitt said it first and best. In his most famous *HBR* article, "Marketing Myopia," Ted argued that most companies suffer from a serious problem with their eyesight. They don't see what business they're really in.

The way the railroads saw it, Ted argued, they were in the railroad business. They didn't see that they were really in the transportation business. A drill company thought it was selling drills. Their customers were actually buying holes.

Ted's article marked the beginning of the idea of reframing, the art of seeing things differently, with your imagination at work. Reframing gives you a valuable tool for thinking, acting, and working with fresh eyes.

The lesson Ted was teaching in 1960 when "Marketing Myopia" came out was a fundamental one: your first job as a leader is to see clearly what business you're in. It's probably not the one you think it is. Which is why you need to take a new look.

That was almost fifty years ago. Today with industry categories collapsing and business boundaries disappearing, reframing itself has been reframed. It's gone meta: the question isn't just "What business are you in?" it's "What's the idea behind the business you're in?"

To borrow from Ted's original example, it's no longer enough for the railroads to say they're in the transportation business. Everyone else, from planes to boats to pieces of the Internet if you're transporting information, is in that business. Some competitors have gone beyond that: FedEx and UPS will deliver a company's packages and move inside the company to manage the whole logistics operation. They'll take a service and turn it into a product or take a product and turn it into a service. That's serious reframing.

Take another transportation provider, Southwest Airlines. It isn't in the airline business or the transportation business. It's in the freedom business—because its low-cost business model and no-frills service yields prices so low we're all "free to move about the country."

If you're a journalist and you think you're in the news business, chances are good you're going to go out of business. News today is a commodity. But there's a good market for the opinion business (think Bill O'Reilly or Keith Olbermann) or even the funny business (think Bill Maher, Stephen Colbert, and Jon Stewart, the last of whom recently finished fourth in the voting for America's most trusted source of . . . news). But none of them is in the news business; they're successful because they are in the ideas-behind-the-news business.

The same kind of reframing applies to Anthropologie: it isn't in the retail business or even the hip fashion and home decorating business. It's in the storytelling business: every store tells a story about the shoppers who associate with an urban, upscale lifestyle with global sophistication and authentically sourced fashion statements. Movie studios aren't in the movie business or even the entertainment business; they're in the branded-experience business, crossing between the big screen with films, the small screen with video games, and no screen with theme park rides, all blended together.

Seeing the idea behind a business comes from the art of reframing. It produces differentiation that not only separates you from your competitors on the basis of your imaginative reframing but also distinguishes those who get it from those who don't.

You can tell the ones who don't get it: they're still selling drills instead of holes. Reframer Home Depot does get it, selling the idea behind the holes—the confidence in your own do-it-yourself skills: "You can do it. We can help." That's the whole idea.

So What?

Some of the smartest business thinkers I know begin their work with the art of reframing. Keith Yamashita of SYPartners teaches companies a model for change that begins, simply enough, with learning how to see; Jim Collins emphasizes the need for great leaders to start out by facing "the brutal facts of life"—in other words, by seeing reality clearly.

Why is seeing so important for business leaders?

Because when you learn to see with fresh eyes, you're able to differentiate your company from the competition. You're able to change the way your company sees the market—and the way your customers see your company.

How do you learn to do it?

Start by asking a different question. Not "What is our product or service?" but "What does our product or service stand for?" A supermarket chain could stand for a healthier life for customers who are willing to pay more for organic food; a coffee shop could stand for neighborliness for the people in its surrounding community who use it as an informal gathering place. Looking through your company to see the values that stand behind it creates a whole new dimension to your business.

Another way to learn: add different points of view. What would an anthropologist say about your company culture? If you invited a cartoonist to draw your business, what would the picture look like? When you invite outsiders in to look at your business you get the benefit of seeing what is all too familiar to you with their new-to-the-scene eyes.

Go visit companies that you think understand the art of reframing. Listen to how they talk about themselves and their customers. Chances are they don't even approach the conversation the way you do.

Here's the real benefit to reframing: it not only helps you see yourself differently, it shows your customers how you see them.

Customers like to do business with smart companies and avoid doing business with dumb ones. When you show your customers that you see them the way they see themselves or, even better, you surprise them with an insight about themselves they didn't realize until you revealed it, they put you in the category of really smart companies. That's the highest compliment a customer can pay you. And it makes it more likely that the customer will keep paying you more than compliments.

THE SYSTEM IS THE SOLUTION.

It's the first law of ecology.

It's the original insight behind the reengineering revolution of the 1980s, started by Michael Hammer.

It's the first discipline in Peter Senge's great book on creating change, *The Fifth Discipline*.

It's deeply embedded in almost all of Michael Porter's work on strategy.

And it's the kind of thinking you'll need to learn if you want to compete and win in the new world of work.

To help you understand why systems thinking is so essential, let me teach you how to start a magazine. You'll see why systems thinking is where it all comes together—or falls apart.

In classical terms magazines are three-legged stools. The first leg is the editorial concept, the idea that's at the center of the magazine. The articles, the writing, and the design all constitute the editorial performance of the magazine. (By the way, there's a system within a system: the words and design need to reinforce each other, down to the choice of paper stock.) The editorial performance enacts the passion and mission of the magazine. It's what attracts the readers.

The readers are the second leg of the stool. You need two things when it comes to readers: the right number and the right kind. The right number depends on the type of magazine you're starting—niche, general interest—and your business model. When I ran *HBR* our readership was around 200,000; at its peak *Fast Company* reached more than 800,000. The number and kind of readers you attract relates back to the first leg of the stool, the editorial product, and also to the third leg, the advertisers.

The advertisers look at your editorial product to see if they like it (or if they even get it). But they look even more closely at your readers: Are they the people they want to reach with their ad pages? Are there enough of them to matter? Do they have the money and the authority to buy the products the advertisers are offering?

In a very simple way the legs of the stool of a magazine are a system. If anything gets out of balance, the stool can easily topple over. Something like 99 percent of all magazines fail in their first year—and that was before advertisers began to relocate to the Web, destabilizing the whole three-legged stool model for all print products.

But when a magazine fails it's fair to say that it's a system failure—which is why leaders have to look at their business not as separate pieces but as an interconnected, interdependent system.

They have to know and obey the laws of the system: Everything relates to everything else. Everything matters.

And if the system works, the whole really is greater than the sum of its parts.

So What?

My point is not really to teach you how to start a magazine.

My point is that embedded in every company, in every organization, is a system. When you see the system and not just the individual pieces you increase your chances of winning.

Most people look at a company and see the organization chart. Or the pyramid of functions. Or the products and services the company offers as output.

Systems thinkers see the relationships, not the functions. They see the processes, not the stand-alone components or the final products. It's the difference between looking at a fence and noticing the barbed wire running horizontally rather than the fence posts standing vertically.

Sometimes it helps to do something as simple as drawing a picture with arrows to show what would otherwise be invisible connections. A drawing of a three-legged stool isn't a sophisticated operations chart, but it makes the point about how magazines need to operate as a system.

Systems thinking can also help when you're trying to solve a perplexing problem. If you want to untangle the clues as to how something went wrong, think like a detective: figure out who all the players are and how they relate to each other. Usually it's the system, not one person or department, that explains the real cause of the problem.

One thing is sure: the future belongs to systems thinkers.

NEW REALITIES DEMAND NEW CATEGORIES.

It took me four years of traveling, listening, and meeting people all over the world before I put the pieces together: *solving today's problems means moving beyond yesterday's outmoded categories.*

I went to visit Oscar Motomura's visionary executive education program in São Paulo and watched him use street theater to teach fifty of Brazil's top business leaders how companies need to incorporate a social mission into their way of doing business.

I went to New York to a national meeting of mayors on the subject of ending homelessness and listened to Louise Casey, who put an end to chronic homelessness under Tony Blair, describe the irresponsible role the military plays in producing—and walking away from—homeless vets.

I went to Detroit to General Motors headquarters and saw firsthand how GM's OnStar system had helped provide relief to victims of Hurricane Katrina who were trapped in their cars.

I went to Singapore and learned that executives from the United States and Europe are resisting being posted to that part of the world because unbearable air pollution constitutes an unacceptable health risk.

The stories are the same everywhere. When we insist on applying the old boundaries between business, government, and not-for-profits all we see is failure.

We see governments unable to come to the aid of their people—whether the crisis is a tsunami in Sri Lanka or a hurricane in New Orleans.

We see companies winning in raw economic terms but losing the confidence of their customers and their own employees because of their lack of social responsibility—whether it's a giant retailer in the United States or a small food producer in China.

We see not-for-profits turning away from old-fashioned philanthropy, which involves supporting people year after year with charity, and instead learning the hybrid art of social entrepreneurship—whether at the Grameen Bank in Bangladesh or Kiva.org in San Francisco.

Today our problems cut across geographical boundaries and organizational categories.

Whose problem is an expensive, underperforming health care system that leaves forty-eight million Americans uninsured? If you stick to the old categories, it's a government problem—but Starbucks reports that it spends more on health care than on coffee beans. That makes it a business problem.

Whose problem is the skyrocketing cost of imported oil? If you take a narrow view of it, energy cost and availability are the auto industry's problems, since U.S. cars account for a stunning 11 percent of total world oil consumption. But energy is the kind of problem that causes wars and economic collapses. That makes it a government problem.

Recently we've seen old categories collapse under the weight of their obsolescence. Governments buy up and bail out failing banks. Companies adopt failing public schools. Not-for-profits launch income-producing businesses, from moving companies to restaurants.

Old lines are blurring and blending. And solutions are becoming more creative, innovative, and effective.

What happens when old categories no longer fit reality?

You can keep trying to cram new realities into old categories. Or you can invent new categories that fit the new realities. One path leads to irrelevance. The other leads to innovation.

So What?

The future will not be kind to people who make category errors.

If you slot your business or organization into the wrong category, if you insist on living within old, no longer relevant categories, you will take years off your life expectancy. If you think you're immune to the economic, social, and political issues that define our time, you make yourself more likely to fail. To win today you need more than peripheral vision; you need 360-degree sight.

If you look at your department or your slice of a company and think that your function alone defines your category, you are setting yourself up to fail.

If you're part of a company that does business all over the world (or just has a Web site, which automatically makes you global) and you categorize your operation within a single nation's boundaries, you are writing your own ticket to extinction.

Instead, when you see a category pop up in front of you, question it. Does it still apply to the way the world works? Or is it a vestigial remain? Recently General Electric CEO Jeffrey Immelt challenged old categories. We used to think about developed and developing nations, he said. But if you fly from Beijing to New York, which airport looks like a developing nation's and which like the developed one's? In fact, Immelt said, GE now organizes the world around new categories: natural-resource-rich countries, people-rich countries, and technology-education-rich countries.

Look for new and emerging categories. If you spot a category before it becomes conventional wisdom, you've got an instant advantage. One example: observers in the United States say we're witnessing the emergence of two new demographic categories, the first since adolescence was invented. One is delayed adulthood, as young people take longer to explore themselves and the world before settling into careers and families; the other is extended seniors, as baby boomers live longer and pursue more active lives.

New categories, new opportunities, new realities.

NOTHING HAPPENS UNTIL MONEY CHANGES HANDS.

This one's for entrepreneurs.

It's true we live in an economy of ideas. Innovation is the watchword for business.

That shouldn't obscure one fundamental fact of life that every entrepreneur needs to internalize: nothing is real until somebody hands you a check. Until then you could have a great idea or a mediocre one, an idea that will reshape an entire industry or disappear without a trace. You'll never know until money changes hands. Then you get to find out.

I learned this lesson when Bill Taylor and I were raising money to test the idea for *Fast Company*. But I didn't learn it from the first check we got; I learned it from the check we didn't get. Here's what happened.

We'd worked over our business plan so many times I'd lost count. We'd gone to friends and experts for advice. We'd had legal papers drawn up and formed a limited liability company. It was time to find our first investor. We'd decided to raise the money in tranches of $50,000. It was a nice round number, and, we thought, a figure our potential backers could afford. I remember practicing my pitch: "You can either buy another new Lexus this year or help launch a magazine."

Our first target: Ted Levitt.

Ted had been my boss; now he was a mentor and friend. He'd retired from *HBR* after reinventing the prestigious if sleepy journal; we'd stayed close after he'd left. As the idea for *Fast Company* developed I made sure he knew about it. It made sense to ask Ted to be our first investor. Plus he had a huge Rolodex filled with successful, wealthy, and influential people around the world. Once Ted was in, we could go to others in his network and ask them for money. He'd be our anchor investor.

When we sat down together Ted took a hard look at our business plan and the legal documents we'd prepared for investors to sign.

"Too much paper," he said.

That was Ted being Ted. He had strong opinions about everything, and they usually started with style points. It mattered to Ted how a presentation looked. It reflected the thinking behind it.

"Why can't it be just a sentence?" he asked. "At most one page. If you want me to invest, that's all it should take."

Bill and I told him he was right, in theory. It would be nice if all we needed was a handshake. But our lawyer advised us that it was good for both sides if we had a formal document. Besides, if he didn't want to read all the legal language, all he had to do was sign the last page.

He told us he'd take a look at it and we left with a warm feeling that we were on our way to our first check for $50,000.

A week went by. No word from Ted. So I called him.

"Haven't had a chance to look at it," he said.

I didn't want him to feel like I was pressuring him. No rush, I told him. I'd wait to hear from him when he was ready.

More time passed. After a while the original warm feeling from that first meeting gave way to something cold and dark. Ted never actually said no to the deal. It just became clear that he wasn't comfortable doing it. I understood. It was his money. He'd been a friend so often in the past, helping in ways large and small, it didn't matter that he never wrote the check.

And he did teach me a valuable lesson: nothing happens, nothing is a deal, nothing is real until money changes hands.

So What?

We all know the expression "Money talks, bullshit walks."

Money does more than talk. It makes things happen. It converts talk to action.

Over the years I've run into two kinds of entrepreneurs. One type loves to talk. They tell you about all the important people who've endorsed their idea. They talk about all the meetings they've had, all the conferences they've presented at, all the people who've promised to partner with them. Most of the time nothing happens with their idea.

Then there are the entrepreneurs who have a short elevator pitch that explains their idea. That's it. After that they're too busy raising money to get their idea launched. They don't always succeed, but they never talk their idea to death.

It's important to remember that money isn't the be-all and end-all, even for entrepreneurs.

But it is the start-all. Especially for entrepreneurs.

So get a sign made and put it on your desk: "The buck starts here."

A GOOD QUESTION
BEATS A GOOD ANSWER.

W hy is a good question so important?

Good question! Jim Collins taught me the answer—or is it the question?

Not long ago I asked Jim what he was working on as a follow-up to *Good to Great*.

"I'm looking for a good question," Jim said.

He explained that both *Built to Last* and *Good to Great* resulted from demanding questions that had challenged Jim to make the most of his powers of research and analysis.

The question behind *Built to Last* was, why do some companies survive and flourish over a long period of time when other companies that appear to be just as competitive go out of business? It took Jim and his coauthor, Jerry Porras, six years to research the question and publish their findings. When the book came out it had a huge impact.

They'd asked a powerful question and embraced it with rigor. In the service of their question they'd willingly thrown away assumptions and preconceptions that could have blinded them. And they'd delivered a set of answers that respected the difficulty posed by the original question and offered actionable advice for serious business leaders.

After the publication of *Built to Last*, Jim, restless soul that he is, began to scout around for a new and worthy question.

One day a consultant friend from McKinsey stopped by for a chat. "Nice job with *Built to Last*," Jim's friend told him. "But there's one problem. *Built to Last* demonstrates how critical a company's original DNA is—its core values and ideology—to its vision and sustainability. But how does that help a business leader who comes to his company long after its founding? What hope is there for a company that doesn't have visionary DNA? How can an existing company go from good to great?"

Now that's a good question. No, make that a *great* question.

After six years of monk-like study, investigation, and analysis, Jim delivered *Good to Great*, and once again changed the way business leaders thought about their jobs.

Why do questions matter more than answers? If you don't ask the right question, it doesn't matter what your answer is. And if you do ask the right question, no matter what your answer, you will learn something of value.

So What?

Questions are how we learn. Which means questions are how we create change.

Why?

Because questions are dangerous. Imagine being alive in the mid-1500s and asking whether the sun revolves around the earth or the earth around the sun. Simply asking the question could change the world—and cost you your life. Sad to say, asking unpopular questions can still be fatal: last year forty-eight journalists were murdered around the world, just for asking questions.

But questions are also liberating. Asking the right question has led scientists to cure terrible diseases, architects to design amazing buildings, and social activists to achieve peace in troubled parts of the world.

Questions are useful. Entrepreneurs and innovators usually start their search for something new and better by asking, "What if?" or "Why not?"

Questions are how we avoid disasters. Groupthink is nothing more than people not asking the questions they know they should.

So why is it so hard for companies to embrace the art of asking good questions?

Much of business is like much of school: the way to get ahead is to make other people think you're smart. The best way to make other people think you're smart, researchers have found, is to make fun of other people when they ask questions. That's also a good way to stop people from asking questions. Over time the purpose of asking questions changes. Instead of looking for new insights, business leaders only ask questions when they already know the answers. Serious questions morph into rhetorical questions designed to reinforce an existing bias or preconception. And it's not just inside companies. Much of what passes for journalism and news analysis is an exercise in asking questions to score debating points.

If you want your company to be committed to innovation,

you need to be a questions company much more than an answers company.

Work at asking great questions in meetings. Reward people for raising questions that need to be asked. Have the courage to ask unasked question to make explicit what you think is obvious—knowing that just by asking the question you'll make new connections and open new lines of inquiry. Decorate the walls of your meeting rooms with sample questions. Capture examples of questions that have made a big difference in solving tough company problems. Practice asking open-ended questions where there is no one right answer.

It's not what you don't know that will hurt you and your business. It's what you don't bother to ask that will kill you.

Asking questions can be dangerous.

Not asking them can be fatal.

Now, any questions?

WE'VE MOVED FROM AN EITHER/OR PAST TO A BOTH/AND FUTURE.

In the old days at Fenway Park, Red Sox fans entertained themselves by swapping chants.

The rowdy crowd in the bleachers started it: "Less filling!"

The folks in the grandstands answered: "Tastes great!"

"Less filling!"

"Tastes great!"

This back-and-forth went on until something happened on the field to interrupt the game between the fans.

The joke, of course, was to mimic the then-popular Miller Lite ads, which featured a pair of retired jocks arguing over what each thought was the real reason to drink the beer.

The ad was fun and smart, in part because of the retired athletes fake-arguing over beer, but also because it mirrored the way the world seemed to work back then: products made you choose. It was an either/or world.

That changed for me when I went to Toyota City in the late 1980s to research a book on Japan's challenge to the U.S. auto industry. It was clear that the Japanese were doing something different and better than the Big Three in Detroit. But what? Was it the role of government in generating industrial policy? The role of suppliers in funneling parts to the automakers? The role of technology and automation in assembling the cars? The role of human resources in motivating the workers? The only way to decode the growing—and perplexing—Japanese advantage was to take a closer look.

As a researcher from the Harvard Business School (HBS), I was accorded open access to the top executives at Toyota and the other automakers. But while the Japanese were unfailingly polite, the interviews I had soon settled into a familiar and uninformative pattern. A uniformed, white-gloved "elevator girl" would escort me to an antiseptic cubicle, serve me a cup of tea, and disappear. Then a polite executive from the automaker would appear. We'd bow, exchange *meishi* (business cards), and begin the interview. I'd go through my strategically designed questions to dig into the various explanations for Toyota's growing dominance: What about the company's relations with its union? With its employees? With the then all-powerful Ministry of International Trade and Industry?

The Toyota executive dutifully recited the same answers he gave all the U.S. interviewers who were flocking to Toyota City seeking enlightenment.

One was that Toyota made sure its employees used their pencils all the way down to the nub before allowing them to ask for a new one.

I dutifully wrote this down. But I was thinking he had to be kidding—or the translation had to be wrong. Toyota was beating Ford, Chrysler, and General Motors because of pencils?

Another was that Toyota had such close relations with its suppliers that parts arrived at assembly plants on a just-in-time basis.

I wrote this down too. But there was nothing new about the just-in-time production system or the Japanese keiretsu structure.

Finally the interview was over and they took me on a tour of an assembly plant. That's when I got it—and in a way that no interview could ever deliver.

The assembly line was where Toyota brought it all together—literally.

I could see the result of human engineering for cost savings coming together with quality engineering for defect-free cars. And the key was, it wasn't one or the other—it was both. Toyota's system produced both high quality *and* low cost. That was the game changer.

In the old game you had to choose. If you wanted high quality, you had to pay a high price. If all you could afford was a cheaper car, you had to accept a lower level of quality. It was one or the other, an either/or world. Toyota eliminated the trade-off. You could have high quality and low cost—a both/and world.

Conventional business strategy turns the world into a matrix with one desirable feature across the top, another down the side: speed versus accuracy, mass versus custom, Web versus print, virtual versus visceral. Conventional business strategists read the matrix in straight lines: you have to choose which feature you're going to favor.

After my visit to Toyota's assembly line I didn't stop making matrices—but I did start reading them on the diagonal. It even helped with our positioning of *Fast Company. HBR* was educational but not entertaining; *Fortune* and the other commercial business magazines entertained you but didn't offer much business education. *Fast Company* cut the matrix on the diagonal: we went into the edu-tainment business.

When F. Scott Fitzgerald said, "The test of a first-rate intelligence is the ability to hold two opposed ideas in the mind at the same time, and still retain the ability to function," he was almost right.

It's actually the test of a first-rate business strategy.

So What?

When you're faced with a tough decision, which do you go with: your head or your heart?

If you chose either one, I'm sorry to say that you missed the point of this rule. Nowhere is it more important than in decision making to embrace the power of the both/and point of view.

Rather than head versus heart, how about using an empathetic head? Or a logical heart?

It takes practice to see the world this way. But one of the skills that defines an entrepreneur and an innovator is the capacity to generate new lines of sight. That means cracking problems open along a new dimension. It means rejecting old either/or choices and finding new both/and syntheses. You learn to do that when you operate on the diagonal. You learn to slice a problem along a new line and then recombine its elements in a fresh way.

One way to practice is to spot both/and examples in everyday life. You can see it when a politician recombines old policy formulations into a new hybrid. Bill Clinton did it when he articulated a "third way" for the Democratic Party. George W. Bush did it when he ran for office as a "compassionate conservative." John McCain captured the idea when he ran for president as a "maverick." And Barack Obama epitomized it when he said there were no red states or blue states—just red, white, and blue states.

You can see it on the business page in reporting on company strategies: competition versus collaboration merges into co-opetition; custom-made versus mass-produced recombines into mass customization. Environmental leaders have long maintained that the perceived trade-off between environmental sustainability and economic growth is a false dichotomy. The combination of environmental imperatives and green technology opens up a future of "green growth."

When you start to operate on the diagonal, you change the game, the way a bishop does in chess. You open up new space; you change the geometry of choice. All it takes is practice and before long you'll start to see the "both" and the "and" in both your work and your life—or your work life.

THE DIFFERENCE BETWEEN A CRISIS AND AN OPPORTUNITY IS WHEN YOU LEARN ABOUT IT.

This is a piece of history—a business parable, really—I learned from Leif Edvinsson, a Swedish friend who is the world's first professor of knowledge management and winner of the Best Brain in the World Award in 1998. Here's the story Leif told me.

For nearly five hundred years, from the 1300s to the early 1800s, the Republic of Ragusa achieved the impossible. This tiny walled city-state on the shores of the Adriatic Sea kept at bay the powerful empires that surrounded it: the Ottoman Empire, the Venetians, and the Vatican. Over the centuries the rulers of Spain and France also posed serious threats to the independent Ragusans.

But somehow, tiny Ragusa, with only five thousand citizens living within its walls, managed to maintain its freedom and achieve an unrivaled standard of living.

How did the Ragusans do it? It's the kind of question that should appeal not only to students of history but also to business leaders seeking to convert old techniques into new sources of competitive advantage.

The answer, it turns out, is knowledge. Ragusa's secret weapon was a knowledge network of highly trained and deeply patriotic ambassadors. By 1800 this network consisted of more than eighty ambassadors deployed by the Ragusan Senate to the courts and ports where their rivals were making important military and economic plans.

These consuls did more than simply represent Ragusa's interests before the all-powerful princes, popes, and pashas who could decide the Republic's fate. The Ragusan Senate regularly sent each ambassador a set of specific questions: What was happening in the shipyard—was a new armada being outfitted? What about the military—was an army being raised? If so, how many troops and what was the name of the general in command? The questions were clear and specific, the information sought purely practical. When the answers came back from the ambassadors the Senate quickly compiled a detailed and accurate picture of the threats and opportunities emerging in the power centers surrounding them.

That was the source of their competitive advantage. Hundreds of years before the creation of the World Wide Web, the Ragusans invented the world's most sophisticated knowledge network. And it was *fast* knowledge. The dispatches that arrived from every corner of the world gave Ragusa's leaders knowledge before anyone else. Knowing more and knowing it sooner meant they had the luxury of time: time to anticipate, to think, to plan. Others, taken by surprise by events, could only react. Ragusa could devise a strategy.

With their diplomatic skills they could play one side off against the other. Or, even better, they could position themselves neatly on both sides of a conflict. In the Battle of Lepanto in 1571, in which the Holy League, comprising Spain, the Vatican, the Venetians, and other Christian forces, defeated the Ottoman Empire, Ragusan boats fought on both sides—for a price.

This proves that there's no such thing as good news or bad news. There's only fast news and slow news. And as far back as 1571, slow news was no news.

So What?

Fast intelligence can sustain a tiny, isolated republic for hundreds of years. Why are so many companies run on the principle of secret hoarding rather than knowledge sharing?

The answer often has to do with an attitude that starts at the top. We all know or have worked for CEOs who proudly proclaim, "We don't have problems! We only have opportunities!"

Actually, they do have problems—sometimes serious ones. And changing the name or pretending they don't exist is both delusional and dangerous. It sends the wrong signal to people operating at the front edge of information, where an early warning system that alerts headquarters to serious problems is an invaluable survival tool. (Ask the Ragusans if you don't believe me.) But inside willfully blind companies the message to those front-line scouts is the same as the first rule of Fight Club: the first rule of Fight Club is you don't talk about Fight Club. The first rule about problems inside intentionally sightless companies is you don't talk about problems.

The second rule of companies-without-problems is never be the bearer of bad tidings to the boss. Inside companies-without-problems, the conventional practice is to shoot the messenger. Companies that say they are striving to adapt to change yet lop off the heads of people who bring important but bad news to the boss are guilty of committing corporate suicide.

The consequences of this kind of self-censorship are frequently fatal. Groupthink and peer pressure on internal dissenters account for historical disasters, from the *Challenger* spacecraft tragedy to the recent ill-conceived U.S. invasion of Iraq. The cautionary tale of the Swedish warship *Vasa* dovetails neatly with the parable of Ragusa—as its mirror image.

The *Vasa*, part warship, part national icon, was built on the orders of the Swedish king Gustavus Adolphus. Built from the finest Swedish timber, the *Vasa* set sail in August 1628. The mighty vessel sailed a short distance from its berth, fired a two-gun salute . . . and promptly sank.

What went wrong?

For one thing, King Gustavus Adolphus redesigned the ship to his own egocentric specifications. By adding an extra gun deck and heavier guns to match a recently built Danish ship, the king introduced changes that were technically unsupportable. No one, however, was willing to argue with the king.

At least the navy conducted a stability test before the *Vasa*'s launch: thirty men ran back and forth on the ship's deck while it was still safely moored. Unfortunately, the men had to stop the test before it was finished—the ship was so unstable, it would have capsized. But the king was waiting for his prize ship, so, despite the failed test, the Swedish admiral approved the launch of the *Vasa*. An estimated fifty sailors drowned when it sank. (Of course, nothing like that ever happens inside companies.)

Today it's hard to imagine any organization that competes on knowledge—whether management consulting firms, ad agencies, law firms, universities, or government agencies— not having a knowledge-sharing capability at least as sophisticated as the one created by the Ragusans centuries ago. If your organization doesn't, create one. If it does have one, improve it: make it faster, more focused, more useful. In times of rapid, dramatic change every company needs an early warning system. The sooner you learn about a crisis, the more time you have to convert it to an opportunity.

LEARN TO TAKE NO AS A QUESTION.

The dinner in San Francisco had been carefully orchestrated. My friend Ernst Scholdan, an Austrian businessperson who delights in supporting iconic projects with social significance, had volunteered to be the first investor in my next change-the-world project. To get the project launched, he figured, we'd form a founders club of a dozen global investors, each of whom would put up $1 million.

The dinner was to close the deal with the second investor, a community-oriented banker who happened to be one of Ernst's closest friends. Which was why every detail of the dinner had to be perfect.

The restaurant had to be chic without trying too hard. Ernst found a traditional San Francisco steakhouse. I knew we were in the right place just from the way it looked. The waiters were pros who'd been there for years. The steaks on display in the meat case were as perfectly aged as San Francisco's wealthiest dowager. Now all we needed was the banker to show up and seal the deal.

This was the fourth time the banker and I had met in mixes of social and business settings. We'd become friendly if not friends. The point of tonight's dinner was to move even closer—$1 million closer.

Everything was perfect, except for one detail.

From the moment he arrived and sat down at the table, the banker's signals made it clear he wasn't working from the carefully prepared script that Ernst and I had rehearsed. We had one version of reality playing in our heads; he had quite a different one in his. And the one in his head, the one that mattered, wasn't interested in putting any money into a project that he understood less the more he heard about it.

"I'm not sure I get this idea," he said. He couldn't have been more generous in spirit, if not in wallet.

I tried explaining it one more time: a global network of thought leaders who could report on grassroots change programs with sustainable business models delivering proven results in addressing pressing social problems. Think of it as the audacity of results, I told him.

"That's all well and good," he said. "But how is this going to help me? Or more importantly, how will my bank benefit?"

I took a deep breath and tried to look at my idea through his eyes. He kept asking questions and I kept searching for the right answers, the ones that would get us back on track toward that $1 million investment. Everything about the evening was just as Ernst had planned it—the food delicious, the wines spectacular—except for one thing: I knew the answer was no.

Afterward Ernst was the one who was disappointed. He'd tried to broker a deal between two friends and it hadn't worked out the way he'd planned. I tried to tell him I'd learned an important lesson. It was a failure on my part, to be sure. But it was also an important learning experience.

The banker was right: my idea needed more work. It wasn't ready. Of course he knew what part he was supposed to have played that night. If he'd done what was expected, he could have taken the easy path, made Ernst happy, and given me a free pass to continue with my fund-raising effort.

Instead he did me an even greater favor. He said no.

He alerted me to the work that I needed to do. He made me confront the fact that I couldn't answer his perfectly reasonable questions to his satisfaction. More importantly, I couldn't answer them to my satisfaction.

In that respect his no was a better investment than a check for $1 million. Not the one I wanted. But the one I needed.

So What?

Businesspeople with an entrepreneurial bent know—or should know—they're going to hear no a lot. As is the case with every disappointment or reversal, the question is what you make of it. Here are a few things to keep in mind when you hear no.

1. **Say thank you.** The correct response to a no is "thank you." True, you didn't get the answer you wanted. But the person who gave you the no also gave you his or her time and attention, listening to your idea and considering it. Now it's your turn. Your job is to show that you've got class and maturity, that you can accept bad news with grace. Chances are good, if you stay in the entrepreneurial orbit, you'll meet this person again.

He or she will remember you more for how you present yourself than for any one idea. Say thank you. You didn't get any money, but with your answer you put money in the bank.

2. Take notes. If the person telling you no offers an explanation, listen carefully, listen respectfully, listen to everything he or she says—without agreeing or arguing. Take out a three-by-five card and write down whatever that individual says. You may have come for money, but these words can be precious gold. You're getting something rare: honest feedback. This isn't a friend telling you what you want to hear. This is an experienced outsider who's giving you a valuable perspective. Write it down—it's exactly what you need to make your idea better.

3. Don't take it personally. Like the man says in *The Godfather*, this isn't personal—it's strictly business. Remember, you went to these people looking for money, not a pat on the head and a hug. They're not saying no to you as a person; they're saying no to your idea in its present form. Don't confuse your idea with yourself. You need to keep some distance between you and your idea—the kind of distance that will let you accept useful criticism about the idea and make it better.

4. All prayers are answered; sometimes the answer is no. Sometimes what you learn from a no is that your idea simply isn't going to work—it can't be made better, it just needs to die. Sometimes someone else is already doing it. Or somebody bigger, stronger, and richer is about to launch his or her version of your idea. Or for reasons you can't explain, you simply can't marshal enough market support for your idea. Some years ago after the successful launch of *Fast Company*, a magazine entrepreneur brought me his idea and wanted to know what I thought. It was a clever idea and there was no reason it couldn't work—except he'd already been at it for three years without much progress. I asked him how much longer he thought he could soldier on. Another two or three years, he told me. My advice: set a date—make it firm and make it sooner than two or three years. If it hasn't happened by then, it isn't going to happen. Putting in more time is only a waste of time. It may be a bitter pill to swallow, it may be the most important learning experience you can have, but at some point there's nothing to do except move on.

Here's the way I thought about it after my dinner with the banker. Learning to take no as a question can be the beginning of a beautiful friendship—with your own idea.

For the first year after I left *Fast Company* I said no to everything.

No to every invitation to give a speech. No to attending any conference. No to every writing offer, job query, business plan. According to my wife, Frances, I spent the year hiding under the covers, decompressing from the ten-year run that was the *Fast Company* story.

But when I got word that Bill Taylor and I had been chosen to receive the Champion of Workplace Learning and Performance Award from the American Society of Training and Development at a conference in Washington, D.C., I couldn't say no to that. It seemed like a safe and easy way to get back into the game after my year of self-imposed exile.

Everything went fine. Bill and I received our awards on the main stage and delivered our thank-yous. Then we improvised a breakout session for about an hour, using themes and stories we'd developed at the magazine: *Fast Company*'s Greatest Hits—the Reunion Tour, but a tour that lasted for one show only. After the session we stood at the front of the room and shook hands with old *Fast Company* friends and fans.

A line of people filtered by until I was face-to-face with a man who introduced himself to me with a thick Arnold Schwarzenegger–like accent.

"My name is Andreas Salcher," the man said, shaking my hand and giving me his business card. "I'm from Vienna, Austria, and I'd like to invite you to speak at a conference we're holding this September at the Abbey at Melk. It's the abbey that was the inspiration for *The Name of the Rose*. We're calling it the Waldzell Conference, from Herman Hesse's novel *The Glass Bead Game*. Our chairman is Paulo Coelho."

He was talking very fast, his accent made it hard to follow what he was saying, and I really wasn't interested. The last thing I wanted to do was to think about flying to Austria to give a speech. I'd come to this conference as a one-time deal and I wasn't about to get back on the old merry-go-round.

"I'll send you an e-mail," he said, and shook my hand one more time.

"Good idea," I said, taking his business card.

That night I emptied my pockets of the notes I'd used at our breakout session and the business cards I'd gotten from friends and well-wishers. The card from the Austrian guy with the faraway conference I tossed in the wastebasket. That was one invitation I could do without.

About a week later an e-mail arrived from Andreas Salcher.

It began, "I know you probably threw my business card away."

That got my attention.

He went over the things he'd told me before: the Abbey at

Melk, Herman Hesse's *The Glass Bead Game*, Paulo Coelho's role.

Then he listed the speakers who'd already agreed to come to the Waldzell gathering: Shirin Ebadi, the Iranian lawyer who'd won the Nobel Peace Prize; Kary Mullis, who'd won the Nobel Prize in chemistry; Günter Blobel, who'd won the Nobel Prize in medicine; Carl Djerassi, who'd invented the birth control pill; Mihaly Csikszentmihalyi, who'd written the influential book *Flow*; Helen Palmer, the world's leading authority on the enneagram; Thomas Hampson, America's leading classical baritone; David Goldberg, the outspoken rabbi of London's leading synagogue; Anton Zeilinger, Austria's leading quantum physicist. The conference was a global dialog for inspiration, with no more than two hundred business leaders in attendance. The theme: our mutual search for meaning in work and our lives. Now would I consider coming as a speaker?

I scanned the e-mail again.

The Glass Bead Game. When we published the beta version of *Fast Company* we included one book review to showcase how creatively we defined a relevant business book. That book was *The Glass Bead Game*, reviewed by futurist Paul Saffo.

Paulo Coelho. I'd just finished reading *The Alchemist*, his celebrated novel on the universal human search for meaning. Now I was invited to speak at a conference he was chairing.

And then the list of Nobel laureates and thought leaders. I had no idea what I could say to add to the dialog—but putting that aside, how could I say no? I had to go.

Here's how it worked out.

I said yes to the invitation. But it was really yes to the experience.

I got to the Abbey at Melk, where I got to meet the other speakers and hear their inspirational stories. I endured several days of low-level panic, not knowing what I would say as the last speaker. At 4:00 A.M. of the morning of my talk, while I was lying in bed staring at the ceiling, inspiration struck. I wrote my talk on a stack of three-by-five cards and later that morning presented my thoughts on the revolutions in science, spirituality, art, and technology represented by the other speakers, culminating in the global business revolution as chronicled by *Fast Company*—my synthesis of the Waldzell gathering. I was invited back the next year as the conference rapporteur and then given the role of chairman of the Waldzell gathering. I made new friends, expanded my global network, gained new knowledge from unanticipated experiences.

But that's not the most important part. After Waldzell, I started saying yes. Yes to giving speeches to gatherings large and small, yes to going on learning journeys, yes to reading other people's business plans, yes to sitting on the boards of nonprofits, yes to doing things where I didn't know what the outcome would be but where the experience promised me a chance to meet remarkable people and encounter new lessons.

Here's what I found. As long as I was open to a new experience, something good always seemed to happen. No matter where I traveled there was always a new person to meet and a new experience to reflect on. I started coming home from trips not with business cards I was eager to discard but with e-mail addresses I was eager to use. All over the world I was meeting people I'd never met before but who were friends as soon as we were introduced. People whom I wouldn't have known if I didn't go.

So What?

Important, busy people live in bubbles. The more important and busy you are, the more time you spend in your own private world. Take the example of one of the CEOs of a leading technology company. Here's what her typical day was like.

She'd be met in the morning at her home by her chauffeur-driven limo. When she got to the office the chauffeur would park in the garage in the special place next to the CEO-only elevator. She'd take the CEO-only elevator to the CEO floor, where several administrative assistants protected her office. Only people with approved appointments made it into her inner sanctum. If she went on a business trip, the limo would drive her to the airport so she could board her private plane. When she landed another limo would meet her and take her to her meetings. Wherever she traveled she was in a hermetically sealed bubble.

Compare that way of doing business to Toyota's *genchi genbutsu* approach. *Genchi genbutsu* translates as "go and see." It doesn't matter whether there's a problem on the factory floor that needs a solution or a need to develop a car to fit a new market. Toyota's principle tells engineers, marketers, or just plain workers on the assembly line to go and see for themselves. No amount of briefings or PowerPoint presentations can substitute for firsthand observation.

"Go and see" flies in the face of today's conventional

wisdom. Businesspeople everywhere habitually complain about information overload: too many e-mails, too many memos, too many meetings. But the real problem isn't too much information. It's too much insulation. The challenge for business leaders is to get out of the bubble that operates as an idea echo chamber.

The truth is, there's no substitute for genuine experience. Ask business leaders about career lessons that have stuck with them and they'll always go back to a key experience that made them get out of their comfort zone—a meeting that was unscripted, a trip that was unplanned, a conversation that wasn't rehearsed. What sticks with leaders is what sticks with all of us—the doing, the seeing, the sharing, the experience. But that means letting go of control and letting new people and experiences penetrate the bubble of security and habit.

Getting out of your comfort zone can come down to things as small as information sources. We all have our favorite magazines, the ones we've been subscribing to for years. What would happen if you went down to your corner magazine stand and bought a stack of new publications that ordinarily you'd never look at? If you're a fan of food, fashion, and travel, take home *Popular Mechanics*. If you're a devoted sports fan, buy *Tin Roof* for a change. If you spot a magazine and you can't imagine why anyone would ever read it, that's the one to buy. Find out for yourself. The same applies to the small circle of friends you always have lunch with or hang out with after work. If you go to the company cafeteria, try sitting down at a table with people you don't already know.

The biggest issue is control. Do you have an admin who

screens your calls and only lets the right people through to you? What would happen if you declared an admin-free day and answered your own phone? Try taking calls you'd ordinarily screen out and see what you learn. Find a conference or lecture to go to that's not part of your regular industry. If you change your point of view and bring back new ideas, you're not wasting time—you're opening up new vistas.

The world is simultaneously a big and little place—big because it's filled with fascinating and even exotic experiences that exceed what we know and encounter inside our own little bubbles, little because everywhere you go you are sure to meet people who are eager to share what they know and to learn from you.

Why stay inside a tight comfort zone when there's so much more to life? Why say no when a simple yes can open up so much?

EVERY START-UP NEEDS FOUR THINGS: CHANGE, CONNECTIONS, CONVERSATION, AND COMMUNITY.

When I think back on all the things I learned from starting *Fast Company*, the mistakes are easy to remember. All start-ups make mistakes, and we made our share. But what made all the difference were the four key things we got right: the 4 C's. They let us stay in the game long enough to fix the mistakes. They're the four things every start-up and any turnaround program in a struggling company need to have. The better job you do with them, the better your chances of success.

Change. The point of a start-up is to change the game—that's the essence of what you have to offer. So your first job is to be crystal clear about what you intend to change in your chosen category. We knew exactly the set of things we wanted to change about business magazines with *Fast Company*. We were going to be the first hip business magazine, a cross between the *Harvard Business Review* and *Rolling Stone*. The design of our business magazine was going to announce our new category: with a cool look and feel we'd make it clear how different we were from the existing stodgy offerings. *Fortune*, *Forbes*, and *Business Week* segmented the market by traditional demographics. *Fast Company* was all about psychographics—we wanted to appeal to businesspeople who saw themselves as innovators and entrepreneurs, change agents and free agents. The other business magazines were unabashedly for business*men*; we recognized the increasing role of women in business and wanted to appeal equally to men and women. We spelled these changes out in our business plan so any potential investor could see the kinds of changes *Fast Company* represented.

Connections. *Fast Company* made two kinds of connections that added energy to our readers' experience: connections between ideas and connections between people. From the beginning, as part of our identity as a different kind of business magazine, we showcased new connections in the world of business thinking. We pointed out the connection between the strategy of war fighting and the strategy of business competition. We introduced readers to a Native American technique for making decisions and invited them to try it at work. We interviewed a brilliant juggler on the concept of balance in work and life, a brain surgeon on the art of handling stress, a pit crew chief on fast turnarounds. By making unconventional connections in a wide variety of disciplines we encouraged our readers to think differently about their work. We also encouraged our readers to connect with each other. Using our Web site as a convener, we encouraged *Fast Company* readers to find each other where they lived: the result was the Company of Friends, a network

of like-minded businesspeople who took the global ideas in
the magazine and made them local. We enabled the connection. They took it from there.

Conversation. The premiere issue of *Fast Company* carried a
letter from the editors intended to serve as our new magazine's manifesto. In it we set out the precepts and principles
of "the handbook of the business revolution" and defined our
purpose: "Start conversations, stimulate debates, provoke
arguments, create healthy tension. *Fast Company* will be the
first—not the last—word in cutting-edge business thinking.
If you find something to apply in your work, something to
talk about with your colleagues, something to help reframe
a problem, something to disagree with, then *Fast Company* is
succeeding." This notion as work as conversation came from
"What's So New About the New Economy?" the last piece I
wrote for *HBR* before I left that magazine to start my own. In
it I argued that in a knowledge economy, standing around
and talking with your colleagues wasn't wasting time—it was
the essence of work. Conversation is how we build on each
other's ideas to create new economic value. At *Fast Company*
every issue aimed to spark new conversations.

Community. To prepare for the launch of *Fast Company* I read
the histories of earlier successful magazines. Here's what
I learned: distinctive magazines not only define an era but
also coalesce a community. In the 1920s the *New Yorker* ca-
tered to an America that was beginning to awaken to its own
sophistication. *Fortune*, when it launched in the late 1920s
defined the new community of business leaders in Amer-

ica as it became corporate. In the 1950s and 1960s *Playboy* served as an arbiter of style for American men as the sexual revolution gained speed. And in the 1960s and 1970s *Rolling Stone* rallied the Woodstock generation to the flag of drugs, sex, and rock and roll. Each magazine succeeded by alerting a group of disparate individuals to the fact that they were, in reality, members of a newly forming community.

I learned the 4 C's from taking a hard look at what we did to put *Fast Company* in a position to succeed—not to guarantee success, but to permit it. But these attributes aren't unique to magazines. If you look carefully, you'll see them working for new business start-ups and new product launches in all kinds of industries. Take, for example, the Obama for president campaign: change, connection, conversation, and community.

So What?

These four words aren't just a cute mnemonic device. They represent a useful surrogate for a more traditional approach to writing a business plan. Try pushing your idea through these four lenses to see how it measures up.

Change. What are you proposing to change about your industry, and in what ways? How will the changes be felt by your customers? At the same time, every new idea has to respect some old traditions. What are you *not* changing? What are you leaving undisturbed so your customers don't feel too disoriented? Change and not-change—that's the first screen your idea has to pass through on its way to improved focus.

Connections. What kind of new connections are you offering your customers? For example, some internal change programs inside companies make a huge contribution by rewiring how information moves, literally reconnecting how work gets done. One of the things the Web enables is new connections between companies and their customers. Procter & Gamble has made a point of harnessing connections in its pursuit of innovation: its new strategy, designed to bring more ideas in from outside the company is even called "connect and develop." What kind of new connections does your idea make?

Conversation. Does your idea start new conversations or take advantage of a dialog with your customers? What kind of feedback loops are you building so your customers—or your employees—can have a genuine conversation? How will you convince your customers that the conversation you're inviting them to have with you is authentic? How will you sustain it after you've started it? For a company or a leader who's sincere about conversation, nothing is more valuable. The voice of the customer is your ultimate guide to success. But you have to mean it; you have to be prepared to listen and respond.

Community. What kind of a community does your idea serve? What are its characteristics? How big is it? And most important, how will you coalesce and serve this community? If you can either serve an existing community or, more powerfully, bring together a new community around your product or service, you'll give your idea an enormous boost. But as with conversation, you've got to be prepared to earn your community's trust—and to trust it. Once your idea empowers a community, it's not your idea anymore—it belongs to the community. You become their supporter, a change many entrepreneurs find hard to accept.

It's easy to use this model as a template for a business plan. Using one piece of paper for each word, explain your idea using that word as a lens. Keep your answers short—one paragraph if possible, one page at the most. Then see how the four pages tie together into a coherent whole. Taken together, change, connection, conversation, and community become a powerful system. If you can harness the 4 C's, you'll give yourself a shot at success.

FACTS ARE FACTS; STORIES ARE HOW WE LEARN.

The place: Registry Resort, Naples, Florida
The date: May 17, 1999
The event: *Fast Company* RealTime conference
The theme: "Are You Ready for the New Economy?"

At 2:45 on the main stage of *Fast Company*'s third Real-Time gathering I introduced our keynote speaker to a raucous crowd of more than six hundred. Management guru extraordinaire Tom Peters came onstage vigorously, energetically—and a little nervously.

He paced the stage and walked up and down the aisles holding a small sheaf of notes, warming up to the theme of this talk.

"Alan said, 'You can't use slides, you can't wear a suit, you can't talk about the things you normally talk about,'" Tom said. Tom was famous for his PowerPoint slides filled with pithy quotes and splashy exclamation points. Today Power-Point was not allowed.

"You're going to think this is insane," he said. "But I had some fun this morning. I spent about a half an hour going through my suitcase. And this is personal, because some of the stuff in there, or the implications of it, is dead flat embarrassing. I'll just dump this crap!"

And with that Tom emptied the contents of a pillowcase he'd brought with him—and the crowd loved it.

Most of them had heard Tom speak before. But not like this! Everybody knew he was a bad boy. He'd charge a company $50,000 or more just to give them a speech about how screwed up they were. But coming out on stage with a pillowcase of stuff from his suitcase? This was seriously cool!

"I'm the wild and wooly guy, right? Crazy? If I'm crazy, why do I carry three watches and wear a fourth one? On top of that," Tom said, lifting up a handful of objects, "I carry not one, not two, but three alarm clocks! That is seven watches and clocks!"

The crowd went wild with laughter.

"There's a message here," Tom said, turning serious. "The message is it's really cool to be cooler than shit. But you also gotta show up on time. This 'Brand You' era, this 'Wow! Project' era is about cool, it's about growth, it's about networking—and it's about a level of accountability that was absolutely not required in corporate halls in years gone by."

He held up two grapefruit-sized balls that had spilled out of the pillowcase.

"Dave Brown made-in-Australia cricket balls," Tom said. "I am an absolutely obsessed design fanatic."

He held up flashlights, rope, a tape measure.

Here's the point: instead of using PowerPoint, Tom told stories. He talked about his mom's influence on him. He spoke of his dad's forty-one-year career spent with just one company—and how thankful he was those days were over. He talked about the two tours of duty in Vietnam that shaped his management philosophy. He talked about false loyalty and empty management goals. The worst thing you can do with your work life, Tom told the crowd, is to live up to the saying "On time, on budget, who cares?"

Tom is always passionate and purposeful. This talk was different.

This time Tom told stories. And stories are how we learn.

Facts are good. Facts can help strengthen an argument. They demonstrate you've done your homework. Here's an example.

In 2008 health care spending claimed 15.4 percent of the United States' gross domestic product. That ranked number one in the world. When it came to child well-being the United States ranked twentieth in the world, behind such countries as Greece, Poland, and the Czech Republic. Those are the facts.

Now let me tell you a story. In late February 2007 in Prince George's County, Maryland, a twelve-year-old boy named Deamonte Driver died of a toothache. Mary Otto wrote in the *Washington Post*: "A routine $80 tooth extraction might have saved him. If his mother had been insured. If his family had not lost its Medicaid. If Medicaid dentists weren't so hard to find. If his mother hadn't been so focused on getting a dentist for his brother, who had six rotted teeth."

Instead, the bacteria from the abscess in Deamonte's tooth spread to his brain and killed him. In the richest country in the world, a twelve-year-old boy living just a few miles from the nation's capital died from a toothache.

Which will you remember? The facts on health care spending? Or the story of Deamonte Driver?

Facts are facts, but stories are who we are, how we learn, and what it all means.

So What?

Have you ever heard of Uncle Ray's Cheddar Popcorn? I hadn't until my wife and I were driving across Iowa on our way to a friend's farm. We stopped at a gas station and bought a bag of Uncle Ray's for a snack. On the front of the shiny blue bag it said, "Chapter 30: Story on Back." After we ate the popcorn I turned the bag over. Here's what it said on the back:

"The Life and Times of Uncle Ray, Chapter 30: Just Peachy." It was a story about Uncle Ray growing up poor in Detroit and a neighbor's peach tree. I won't ruin it for you by telling you the whole story—but like Tom Peters' speech at RealTime, it was personal, it was compelling, and it had a very poignant morale. It was every bit as good as the popcorn, maybe better.

Does putting a story on the back of a bag sell more popcorn? Or is it just Uncle Ray's way of giving something back, a little life lesson with every serving? Doesn't matter—I loved the popcorn so much I ate it all and I loved the story so much I kept the bag.

Why are stories so much more powerful than plain old facts or boring PowerPoint presentations?

For one thing, stories are about people. People relate to other people. People don't relate to bullet points, cold numbers, charts, or graphs.

Stories are about people doing things. That means stories have verbs. Verbs are important—they define something that is happening, has happened, will happen, or should happen.

Verbs are specific: when a good storyteller is spinning a tale, it's the verbs that convey important distinctions and subtleties. Numbers, charts, and graphs appear to be specific, but without verbs it's hard to know what the numbers actually mean. The numbers may look "hard," but they're actually soft. Stories may appear "soft," but the verbs make them hard. Counterintuitive, that, but it's how stories work.

Stories create meaning. Data are fine, but what we crave is some way to make sense out of all the numbers. We look to stories to tell us how to organize the facts so they mean something.

Stories are how we learn. Embedded in every story are lessons about life. Stories offer instruction on how to behave, what courage looks like, how to come to terms with disappointment, and what it means to build character. They're how we pass on to others what we've learned.

Stories have always been at the heart of starting and leading companies. Most start-ups have creation myths. Some track back to a garage, some to a dorm room at a university. They all convey the founder's values, purpose, and character. (If you're starting a company and you don't have an actual creation myth, feel free to make one up—that's what we did at *Fast Company*.)

Most companies celebrate their great successes and even their heroic failures in stories, like ancient tribes passing on the tales of previous generations: the most amazing sales victory ever achieved, the contract the boss walked away from because it involved dishonesty, the time everyone pulled an all-nighter to beat the competition. Stories transform a company into a community. They create legend and lore and inspire people to work harder, work together, and work with meaning.

The work of leading a company is the work of telling stories. It's an art, but it's an art that can be learned.

First, check your PowerPoint at the door. You won't miss it, I promise.

Then think about the lesson—the real message—you're trying to convey. That goes at the end of your story—that's the moral of your tale. Then work your way from the end back to the beginning, until you reach the place your story naturally begins: "Once upon a time . . ."

You'll discover a new ability, a way of organizing and describing your experiences so that they connect with others' experiences. People will listen. And you'll never have to suffer through another mind-numbing PowerPoint presentation again—unless someone else is giving it.

ENTREPRENEURS CHOOSE
SERENDIPITY OVER EFFICIENCY.

If you go to Portland, Oregon, these days as a tourist you're in for a treat. A light rail line whisks you from the airport to the city center, where Pioneer Square, a vital one-block park, welcomes you to America's most walkable downtown. Unlike most downtowns in the United States, Portland's is flourishing, alive with mixed uses, street vendors, fountains, parks, and plazas. A transit mall runs the length of the downtown, and within the "fareless square" you can even ride for free. Running the length of the waterfront is a huge public park, and in the Pearl District are midrise condominiums, hip new restaurants, cool shops, historic buildings, and, if you ever get bored, Powell's Books. It's a great city center.

It wasn't always like this.

In 1973 downtown Portland violated federal air pollution standards one day out of three. What is now Pioneer Square had been slated to become another parking garage. What is now the waterfront park was a waterfront freeway. The Pearl District was warehouses. There was no vibrant downtown. The city's one urban renewal district consisted of a series of dull poured-concrete high-rise apartment buildings ringed by a moat of cars. Downtown Portland, like most American downtowns, had been dedicated to the automobile, with the notion that the easier it was for cars to come into the central city, the more likely it was that people would shop there. The truth was, cars were killing the downtown.

The auto was the issue that divided the city. The old guard believed in the car: they wanted to bulldoze houses to build more freeways to move cars through the city's neighborhoods and they wanted to build more parking garages downtown to house the cars. They wanted to widen streets, cut down street trees, do whatever was needed to maintain the efficient flow of cars through the city.

The young Turks in city hall working for Neil Goldschmidt and the activist citizens in Portland's neighborhoods thought cars would mean the death of the city. We wanted to emphasize transit, preserve neighborhoods, and make downtown more pedestrian-friendly.

The confrontation between the two sides came down to the Downtown Plan, a comprehensive planning effort to chart the future of the city's center. The city council hired professional consultants, urban planners, and transportation experts to do the official planning. It also appointed a citizens' advisory committee to draw up a list of guidelines. My job? The mayor made me his liaison to the citizens' advisory committee. I was supposed to help guide the citizens who were drawing up the guidelines.

Only I knew nothing about urban planning. I'd grown up in the suburbs of St. Louis and gone to college in western Massachusetts. I'd studied reading and writing and put out the college newspaper. When it came to urban planning I was a blank.

If I was a perfect cipher, there was a perfect solution. They handed me the perfect textbook: *The Death and Life of Great American Cities*, Jane Jacobs' masterpiece on how cities work. It turned out she hadn't been a city planner or transportation expert; she was a citizen, a gifted amateur who used her own experiences to shape a compelling theory of how to save a city. Her book became my bible.

She talked about the importance of mixed uses downtown, how segregating downtowns into sterile clusters, like a traditional government center, can kill a downtown. She explained how short city blocks translate into great pedestrian experiences, talked about the importance of retail uses at the street level of office buildings, and described why plazas and setbacks produce dead spaces at the street level that suck the life out of cities.

And in one powerful chapter she outlined perfectly the battle that was going on in Portland: cities either experienced the erosion of the city by the automobile or the attrition of the automobile by the city. In that contest the city's future hung in the balance.

So What?

What I didn't know at the time and only came to appreciate later after I moved away from Portland was that I'd received a lesson not only in urban planning but also in entrepreneurship, in two important ways.

First, the contest for Portland's future was a prototypical business battle. Those favoring the status quo were defending the traditional business model, the one that had governed the fate of most American cities. In fact, it was more about suburbs than cities, more about cars than neighborhoods, more about social and economic divisions than community development. Those of us advocating the alternative path were urban entrepreneurs. We had a different business model, one that emphasized neighborhoods, livability, environmental quality, transit, and citizen engagement as the underlying values. The two sides couldn't compromise; there was little middle ground on which to agree. The city had to make a political choice, either for the status quo or for the entrepreneurial vision. It was raw business model competition.

Second, underlying the political divide was a philosophical choice, one that I later realized also separates managers from entrepreneurs. It's a split between habit and surprise, between familiarity and discovery, between safety and risk, ultimately between efficiency and serendipity.

Managers favor efficiency. Efficiency builds freeways and parking lots. Efficiency bulldozes neighborhoods and surrenders cities to automobiles. Efficiency resists change because change introduces friction and friction adds costs. Efficiency takes the same route to and from work every day—because it's simpler, easier, and eliminates the need to pay attention.

Entrepreneurs favor serendipity. The same things that make cities fun, exciting, and vibrant places draw entrepreneurs to innovation and experimentation. Entrepreneurs want to know, "What's around that corner?" They don't want to take the same route to work every day; they want the freedom to explore new paths and discover new experiences. Entrepreneurs are the Jane Jacobses of business: they're looking for short blocks and street-level retail, sidewalk cafés and pushcart vendors. They're hungry for fresh encounters with daily life that offer the opportunity for moments of insight and inspiration or just plain joy.

Imagine that, like Portland in the early 1970s, you're at a crossroads, a personal inflection point. Which business model will you choose for your life? Will you favor efficiency and stick with the road well traveled? Or will you strike out in a new direction, blaze your own trail, and choose serendipity?

"The point of cities," says Jane Jacobs in *The Death and Life of Great American Cities*, "is multiplicity of choice." That's also the point of entrepreneurship.

KNOWING IT AIN'T THE
SAME AS DOING IT.

I first met Larry Smith at a political conference born out of utter defeat.

In 1980 Ronald Reagan buried Jimmy Carter in a landslide, 489 electoral votes to 49. A group of us had gone from Portland, Oregon, to Washington, D.C., to work with Neil Goldschmidt when he was named secretary of transportation. Now we turned around and trudged back home, with Tip O'Neill's famous saying ringing in our ears: "All politics is local." Oregon hadn't gone Democratic in a presidential election since 1964. We decided we'd organize an Oregon–Washington State forum of young Democrats, fifty from each state, to begin the long rebuilding process from the grassroots up.

My task was to find two speakers to kick off the conference, one on economics, one on national defense. I finally found them: Alan Blinder, at that time a Princeton professor and a rising star among Democratic economists; and Larry Smith, a relatively anonymous Washington, D.C., staffer whose fingerprints seemed to be on every new idea dealing with national security.

The gathering on Mt. Hood was a terrific success; Alan Blinder sketched out a Democratic economic vision that later resurfaced in the Clinton administration, where he served as a member of the Council of Economic Advisers. Larry Smith, who went on to be counselor to the secretary of defense in the Clinton administration, dazzled us with a plainspoken explanation that put our national defense in commonsense terms: when it comes to defense spending, Larry said, more isn't better, less isn't better, only better is better.

More importantly, Larry became a friend for life. But the most profound lesson I've learned from Larry didn't come up on Mt. Hood; it's a sentence he used to write on the white-board at the Kennedy School of Government, where he taught for years: "Knowing it ain't the same as doing it—old Hoosier saying." Even though Larry worked in Washington, D.C., for more than thirty years and ended his government career with the Defense Department's highest civilian honor, he never forgot where he grew up: Dayton, Indiana, a town so small, Larry likes to say, it's not even the county seat.

What's so important about this piece of down-home Hoosier wisdom?

First, it has to do with who you listen to. Washington, D.C., is a city of experts. There are experts in think tanks who write policy papers, experts who testify in front of congressional committees, expert pundits who occupy the airwaves, and even expert pundits who interview other expert pundits in an endless echo-chamber effect of expert punditry.

Something has changed in America in all of this, and not for the better. In an economy of ideas, theory has trumped practice. People go to Washington, D.C., to hold a high office, not to accomplish anything. Thinking has replaced doing. The same is true in business. An executive with a prestigious job title can claim an impressive resume. Actually doing something to go with the title seems almost beside the point.

The second lesson has to do with knowledge. It's table stakes to say we live in a knowledge economy. The real question is, what kind of knowledge is most valuable?

There are two ways of knowing. One way comes from the head. It's the kind of knowing that comes from reading and thinking—it's the kind of theorizing that experts excel at. The other way of knowing comes from doing. Unlike the first form of knowing, which starts in the head and stays there, this form of knowing starts in the hands and moves up to the head and then back down again in a knowing-doing loop.

In his years in Washington, D.C., Larry saw both kinds of knowing. In the Defense Department he worked with sophisticated theoreticians who'd derived their ideas from ideology rather than real human experience. As a political operative, he dealt with high-paid consultants who'd never actually talked with a cop, a union member, a farmer, or any other real live voter. In matters large and small, Larry saw, we've lost touch with a time-honored American value: real experience. That loss has real consequences: as we try to solve difficult problems we've moved farther away from their roots. What we need is a return to the real world, with close observation at the grassroots level and applied knowing gathered from real experience.

Knowing in the abstract ain't the same as doing in practice—but doing, it turns out, can open up whole new ways of knowing.

So What?

We all love experts. They're so smart and reassuring to have around. But the problem comes inside companies when a culture of knowers overwhelms a culture of doers.

In your company, who gets listened to when it comes to assessing an idea or evaluating a project? If your company is like most, good talkers get taken more seriously than real doers. To get an idea considered in most organizations you need to be able to make a crisp presentation with PERT charts, bar charts, pie charts, and flip charts. The people in the field who are closest to the problem and closest to the customer may be useful when it comes time to do what our experts have advised. But let's leave the thinking to the people at the top, the executives and their consultants tucked inside headquarters. For that matter, as they make their way up the ranks, too many business leaders lose touch with the real work that formed their real business education. They don't do what they used to be so good at doing; instead, they make decisions that tell others what to do.

If you've made it to the ranks of business thinkers, here's something to think about. As a leader, what kind of advice do you seek, whom do you seek it from, and what kind of evidence do you ask for? There are undoubtedly plenty of smart consultants out there. But don't forget: you've got plenty of street-smart frontline people in your own organization, men and women who are close to the customer and have deep working knowledge about what works and what doesn't in your company. How do you get access to their kind of knowing, the kind that comes from actual doing?

How do you tell the difference between an idea that sounds

good in theory and one that works in practice? Do you use "stress tests" (Larry Smith's words) that will tell you whether an idea can actually hold up under pressure? Do you look for battle-tested project captains who have the scars to show for the time they've devoted to making things happen? How do you reward not only good thinking but also good experience? Do you make heroes out of the men and women who have the courage to try to implement an idea—whether it succeeds or fails—rather than talking it to death?

Success is built around finding what works and why. It comes from empirical evidence, not theory. Success comes from having answers you can trust and believe in—and to get those answers you have to go beyond just knowing. You have to go to just doing.

MEMO TO LEADERS: FOCUS ON THE SIGNAL-TO-NOISE RATIO.

The businessperson with the thick Austrian accent wasn't familiar with one of the speakers who'd been scheduled for the third Waldzell gathering.

"Warren Bennis," I explained to her, "is the world's foremost authority on leadership."

The woman gave me a skeptical look. "Leadership," she said. "We've had bad experiences with that in this part of Europe."

Europe may have had bad experiences with leadership, but in America we've suffered from bad definitions of leadership—and in a country that genuinely values leadership, bad definitions only produce more bad leaders.

Two definitions have dominated the way the business press has described leadership: the macho CEO and the decider in chief. For decades leadership in business was synonymous with toughness. Every year *Fortune* magazine published a cover story naming "the ten toughest bosses in America." Leadership, according to *Fortune*, could be found at the corner of kick ass and take names. More recently that macho-to-the-max definition gave way to the notion of the decisive CEO, the great man (almost always a man) who sat behind the big desk making the big decisions. This CEO wasn't just tough—he also had to be the smartest guy in the room, any room.

We can be thankful that the first version of leadership has expired, as more and more CEOs have learned that smart, talented people—the kind who make a great business run—are unwilling to work for a jerk. The second version is on its way out simply because it's increasingly unrealistic to expect any CEO to know more than everybody. "None of us is as smart as all of us" is a mantra more and more CEOs are learning.

Which leads to the question: What is the right way to think about leadership today? Or, to turn the question around, what is the organizational problem that leadership needs to solve?

The problem today is too much information sharing and not enough sense making: too many messages, too many meetings, too many e-mails, too many change programs, too many changes in direction. The problem only gets worse when the stakes go up—when a company is facing a crisis, when it's up against an innovative competitor and the old ways won't work. That's when too many leaders give in to the temptation to ramp up the volume and amp up the adrenaline. The result: an already overtaxed system collapses from overload.

The answer is where real leadership lives today: leaders need to provide more signal and less noise. If you're a leader, your people need three things: clarity about purpose, honesty about values, and focus about metrics.

They need to see what you see. Tell them what really matters. Tell them how to make sense out of all the conflicting reports and swirling rumors. Tell them how you connect the dots so they can see the pattern you see. That way they'll have your template to guide their actions.

They want to know what you feel. Tell them what the company stands for. Make an uncompromising statement of the code of conduct that guides your organization. Then live by it yourself and hold them to it. They'll rally to that kind of leadership.

They want to track what you measure. Tell them the few things that really matter when it comes to measuring performance—as few as possible. Too many things to measure and you're back adding noise, not signal.

That's the definition of leadership: ramping up the signal and damping down the noise, making sense out of confusion. If you do that job as the leader, you'll make it possible for your people to do theirs.

So What?

I owe this definition of leadership to four different teachers, each of whom contributed an important component. The term "signal-to-noise ratio" comes from John Seely Brown. When I met him he was the chief scientist at Xerox Corporation and director of the Palo Alto Research Center (PARC). A signal-to-noise ratio is an electrical engineering term: it's a ratio of the power of a signal to the power of the noise that is corrupting the signal. The higher the ratio, the clearer your message.

From the unassailable Peter Drucker I learned that the job

of a manager is to allow workers to do their jobs to the best of their ability—not to hinder their efforts with useless managerial interference. It was Drucker who first emphasized the social side of business and the human side of management.

Jim Collins adopted Peter Drucker's thinking and then refined it as only a trained mathematician could. In *Good to Great*, Collins teaches leaders to think like hedgehogs, not foxes: every company that made the leap from good to great had a leader who could express the company's purpose in a single short sentence. It's not breadth of vision that defines good-to-great leaders but clarity of focus.

And from Stanford's Jeffrey Pfeffer I learned an important improvement on the old management saw that what gets measured is what gets done. That's true, Pfeffer found—except when a leader insists on measuring too many things simultaneously. Too much measurement is no different from no measurement at all. Pick a few metrics that matter and stick to them.

Those are four all-star leadership teachers. But how do you put their lessons to work for you?

First, begin with a moment of self-assessment. What is your operating definition of leadership? Do you have one? Did you formulate it yourself, read it in a book that influenced you, or learn it from a mentor who taught it to you? Write it down. What does it say about your relationship with the people who work for you? What does it describe as your key set of tasks? Does it make you a motivator, a decider, a sense maker?

Second, do another assessment, this time of your organization. What defines your company and your way of doing business? Can you boil it down to a few words? Nordstrom's guide to its employees is legendary for its succinctness. When Gordon Bethune turned around Continental Airlines, he gave his team two words to focus on: *dignity* and *respect*. Can you be as focused as a hedgehog?

Third, what are your company's values? Marvin Bower, the man who is credited with making McKinsey & Co. what it is today instilled four key values into the fledgling firm: clients come first; engagements should only be taken when the value to the client exceeds the fee to the firm; active partners should own the firm; members of the firm should be professionals with the training and motivation to do outstanding career work. Four values. Can you name yours?

Fourth, what are your key metrics? And how can you keep the number of things you measure to the absolute minimum?

Do this simple assessment and I guarantee you'll boost your signal-to-noise ratio. And make more sense.

B efore I tell you about the ideas in John Boyd's book let me describe the book itself.

It's about an inch thick with a puke-green cover and a flimsy plastic spiral binding. Everything about it says homemade. Its pages are nothing more than photocopies of hundreds of slides from a presentation. On the cover it says in all caps, *A DISCOURSE ON WINNING AND LOSING*. Under that in letters so small they are easy to overlook it says, "John R. Boyd, August 1987."

I treat this cheesy-looking book with the utmost respect because, as bad as it looks, it is one of the most influential works on strategy ever written. It looks like a spiral-bound version of a slide deck because that's exactly what it is: a legendary presentation that changed the Pentagon's thinking about military strategy in the 1980s, written by a man who almost single-handedly reimagined the design of American fighter places and reinvented American military campaigns. By the time I got my hands on this book the thinking in it had already migrated from military strategy to corporate strategy, where the elegant and practical ideas found a new and eager audience.

I got my copy of this priceless collector's item from Tom

Hout, one of the Boston Consulting Group's most creative strategists. In the 1980s and 1990s Tom and George Stalk, his thinking partner, were tracking new ways to compete. George was in Japan trying to figure out how the manufacturers there were able to bring so many new products to market so quickly. Tom was fascinated by the new direction military strategy was taking in the United States. They merged their inquiries in a new kind of strategy that they called time-based competition—but that's getting ahead of the story.

Because the real story is John Boyd. John Boyd was the maverick's maverick, an exceptional fighter pilot and an instructor of fighter pilots. *A Discourse on Winning and Losing* is a synthesis of everything he first learned and then taught about how to triumph in combat, a tour of warfare that starts with Lao Tzu and ends with modern guerilla campaigns. In the end what Boyd produced is a compelling and comprehensive textbook on how to win in any kind of engagement, whether military or commercial.

According to Boyd, all conflict can be divided into three types: attrition warfare, maneuver conflict, and moral conflict. Boyd prefers maneuver conflict and its attributes or operational style: ambiguity, deception, novelty, fast and transient maneuvers, and economy of effort. What he particularly likes is the way maneuver conflict disorients, disrupts, and overloads the enemy: you win, Boyd says, by "folding the enemy back on himself." With his mental images of the conflict disoriented, his operations disrupted, and his internal harmony destroyed, the enemy surrenders, having lost the will to fight. It's a brilliant grand synthesis, combining the lessons of history's greatest military minds.

But how do you implement this strategy?

This is Boyd's unique and useful insight—and the source of his nickname, "Forty-Second" Boyd.

At the heart of all competition—all life, Boyd argues—is the OODA loop. *OODA* stands for *observation, orientation, decision, action.* According to Boyd, the OODA loop is the process that describes how we make the decisions that govern all winning and losing, in war, in business, in life.

But understanding the OODA loop is only the first step in winning at competition. The key is that whoever goes through the four steps of the OODA loop faster gains the advantage. If you can move from observation to orientation, from orientation to decision, and from decision to action while your rival is still stuck at one of the earlier steps, you will win. As you cycle rapidly through the stages of the OODA loop you quickly put your competition on the defensive; you sow doubt, mistrust, confusion, fear, and panic inside the enemy. Your ability to make decisions and take action will outmaneuver the enemy—it makes all the difference between winning and losing.

To Boyd the OODA loop was more than theory; it was his weapon of choice in combat. As an Air Force flight instructor, Boyd issued a standing challenge to any student. In aerial combat Boyd would start at a positional disadvantage and in less than forty seconds he would outmaneuver the student and win the dogfight. Boyd never lost the challenge and earned his nickname—because he had mastered the strategic art of the OODA loop. Speed, he proved, is strategy.

So What?

When competition in business was based on mass production, mass marketing, and mass consumption, attrition warfare made sense. It was like the Civil War: you could wear down the competition by using superior scale and scope.

But what happens when the game changes? When ideas and knowledge, innovation and creativity, variety and flexibility become the new qualities you need to compete? When competition shifts from attrition warfare to maneuver conflict?

That was the question Tom Hout and George Stalk asked in the 1980s as Japanese manufacturers of cars, air conditioners, stereos, and other consumer electronics swamped U.S. producers with more variety, higher quality, and lower costs. How were they able to do it?

The answer, they found, was speed. The answer was the OODA loop, applied to business.

How does it work? Let's walk through the steps of the OODA loop.

Observation. How acute are your powers of observation? All companies like to think of themselves as keen observers; but just as some armies have better scouts than others, some companies work harder at scanning the competitive landscape than others. For instance, technology-driven companies routinely map the patents their competitors file—not only to see what the new applications address but also to detect patterns that suggest broad new areas of interest. Other companies use scenario planning or simulation exercises to game possible alternative futures. How do you scout

out change before it occurs? Do you have people and practices in place that let you observe and analyze your customers' migrations and your competitors' strategies?

Orientation. According to Boyd, orientation is the key step in the whole OODA loop. He calls it the *Schwerpunkt*, or focal point, because it "shapes the way we observe, the way we decide, the way we act." Orientation means making sense out of what you observe. It requires self-knowledge to avoid falling into the trap of complacency; it demands self-awareness to avoid falling prey to mind-numbing habit. What are your habits of mind that shape how you make sense of experience? What are the preconceptions that color your observations about how the world really works? You may not even know what assumptions you're making, much less whether they apply to a rapidly changing world. Making them explicit is why orientation is a key step in the process.

Decision. What is your speed of decision making? Are you quick to decide? Or do you get trapped in analysis paralysis? The OODA loop emphasizes swift and committed decision making. It also has a built-in self-correcting mechanism: your first decision may not be perfect, but as you rapidly go back through the cycle of the OODA loop you get a chance to improve your first decision. With every turn of the cycle your decisions get faster, clearer, and better.

Action. It's not enough to decide; nothing happens until you convert your decision to action. Companies that embrace the OODA loop know that time is the key metric. How long does it take to move from decision to action? How many layers can you eliminate to speed up the process, how many obstacles can you remove to show your commitment to action? One approach is to appoint a "speed team" that follows a decision through the organization all the way to implementation. At the end, you'll know where the holdups are—and how to get rid of them.

What happens next?

You go through the cycle again and again, observing the impact of your first round, orienting yourself to the emerging situation, deciding what needs to be done differently, and acting to make it happen. The OODA loop becomes a strategic discipline, clocking the speed with which you create and implement strategy and the speed with which you learn how to adapt to a fast-changing competitive environment. In a knowledge economy speed is the critical measure and learning the most valuable skill.

GREAT LEADERS ANSWER TOM PETERS' GREAT QUESTION: "HOW CAN I CAPTURE THE WORLD'S IMAGINATION?"

The evidence is there for all of us to see. It's in the newspapers, on TV, on the Web—companies announcing their innovation intentions to the world.

A two-page spread in the newspaper heralds Coca-Cola's great leap forward: a variety of shapes, sizes, and designs of cans and bottles offering us . . . the same fizzy water in a bunch of slightly different containers.

A series of ads in popular magazines trumpets Delta Airlines' new campaign to win the hearts and minds of the flying public with its innovations. One ad features the option of checking in online before you leave home . . . which every other airline also lets you do.

A thirty-second spot for Sprint running on TV makes charming use of an attractive couple seated at an outdoor café, each using an innovative cell phone . . . which has a mirror on the back.

Wow! Talk about innovation! Talk about differentiation!

Some companies go for the gold when it comes to new products and services.

But not many.

Most companies play it safe and call it innovation. Most companies make an incremental packaging change and call it a breakthrough. They benchmark their competitors and look for small ways to make big claims. They say they're reaching for the sky—and then settle for the next-to-the-top shelf in the garage where the old gear gets stored. It's safe. Nobody gets fired for predictable mediocrity. Just don't call it innovation. It's more like mini-vation.

Which is where Tom Peters' fist-shaking challenge hurled at both fresh-eyed entrepreneurs and flinty-eyed corporate types comes in.

"Dammit!" Tom shouts. "Enough of this weak stuff! Now's the time to capture the imagination of the world! And if not the whole world, at least *your* world!"

We all know what Tom's talking about. We all know "lame" when we see it—and we all know "it" when we see it.

If you wear a thin yellow bracelet around your wrist that says "LiveStrong" on it—or any colored bracelet that represents a cause you care deeply about—you saw "it." What started out in 2004 as a symbol developed by Nike and Wieden+Kennedy to generate contributions to the Lance Armstrong Foundation turned into a global statement. It took six months for the campaign to reach its original target of raising $25 million by selling bracelets at $1 apiece. To date people all over the world have bought more than seventy million yellow bracelets.

If you saw the Nomadic Museum created by Japanese architect Shigeru Ban to house Gregory Colbert's "Ashes and Snow" traveling photo exhibit, you saw "it." Ban built a movable Japanese temple out of metal rail cars, recycled columns, and black rocks. After the exhibit closed at each stop the rail cars became shipping containers to move the show to its next destination.

If you read any of the seven Harry Potter novels or saw one of the movies or played one of the video games, you saw "it." Here's a story that seems at first glance a mash-up of time-honored British boarding school romances, traditional coming-of-age stories, and return-of-the-hero sagas—which might explain why eight publishers told J. K. Rowling no before one took a chance on the young wizard. To date Harry has sold more than four hundred million copies, been translated into sixty-seven languages, and spawned a Potter empire valued at more than $15 billion while inspiring millions of young people all over the world to do something everyone knows kids don't do anymore: read a book.

We all know it when we see it. It's in the iPod and iPhone, in Camper shoes, and the "Bangle butt" of BMWs. It shows up in Web sites with something to say, in kitchen products that are easy to use, in social businesses that work and make a difference. You can capture the world's imagination with a drive-in hamburger joint that features a secret menu, with a pen that writes upside down, or with a book that's printed on a nonpaper recyclable material. You can do it for money, for a cause, or, if you publish a fake issue of the *New York Times*, just for a laugh.

The point is, capturing the world's imagination is the only game that's really worth playing.

So What?

What does it take to capture the world's imagination? Take a look at the examples you're familiar with. What do they have in common?

Courage, to start with. It takes guts to try to do something "insanely great," as Steve Jobs once put it. You have to know you'll be criticized, maybe even mocked, for being different, for breaking the rules, for listening to yourself instead of listening to "them."

That calls for commitment. You have to be so committed to your project you can't imagine *not* doing it. It's actually the opposite of that famous saying from the Apollo 13 space rescue: failure is an option—but not trying is unimaginable.

It takes clarity. There is a crystal clarity to the projects that capture the world's imagination. When you pick up an OXO kitchen product you know instantly that the defining purpose of this humble piece of kitchenware is to redefine the user's cooking experience. The LifeStraw water purifier is literally crystal clear: it transforms any kind of surface water into safe, clean drinking water. You hear about this kind of clarity from Nobel Prize laureates who say they'd been thinking about a problem for years, only to have the solution appear to them in a dream. Like chance, clarity favors the prepared mind. It takes years of work to produce the overnight success that captures the world's imagination through its clarity.

Simplicity is part of the equation. Think of the steps an architect goes through to take an idea that's clear and refine it into an idea that's also simple. When Bill Taylor and I were writing the business plan for *Fast Company* we went through dozens of iterations. The clarity of the idea never changed; the simplicity with which we could describe kept improving. Simplicity strips away components you don't really need. Your project becomes more itself. As it becomes more itself it becomes more of a presence in the world.

Finally comes flawless execution. Every choice, every decision, every expression of the idea matters. Why did it make sense for the LiveStrong band to be yellow? How did Frank Gehry settle on titanium sheathing for his Bilbao museum? You only get one first chance to capture the world's imagination. How prepared are you to get each detail right?

And if it doesn't work? If the world shrugs at your effort to capture its imagination? If you get criticized or ignored? If you fail?

The truth is, mediocre innovations succeed every day. Courageous, committed, clear, simple, and flawlessly executed innovations fail just as often.

So here's the question: Would you rather have a tepid success with something that doesn't matter or a brilliant failure with something that does?

My advice is to keep Tom's question ringing in your ears. It's the best question I've ever run into. It's a challenge for all of us to play the game to the best of our ability, at the peak of our powers, and at the height of our passion.

LEARN TO SEE THE WORLD THROUGH THE EYES OF YOUR CUSTOMER.

My father was a great salesman.

I didn't learn this until after he died and people from all over St. Louis—all over the country, in fact—made it a point to tell me what my dad had meant to them. And those were his customers talking.

The confusing part of this for me was that when I was growing up, my dad had always maintained that he hated business. He'd wanted to be a history professor. He was only a few credits short of getting his master's degree when his father died and he left school to do whatever he had to do to support his mother and the younger kids in the family. When World War II came he joined the Army. After it ended, my multitalented mother taught him how to take pictures. Until he retired he was a camera salesman who wanted to be a historian.

So if he hated business, what made him a great salesman?

He loved people. Mostly he loved helping people. If a customer had a big family vacation coming up or just a weekend barbeque, my dad would loan him a camera and teach him how to use it, no strings attached. But it wasn't just cameras. He had a customer who loved peaches, so he'd drive over to Illinois and bring back a bucket of farmstand fruit. Another customer had kids who were Cardinals fans, so he'd bring them T-shirts, key chains, anything with a red bird on it.

The company he worked for, which went from Stanley Photo to Fox-Stanley Photo to Fox Photo, was selling cameras, film, and photo finishing.

The customers, which included Anheuser-Busch, Monsanto, Ralston Purina, McDonnell-Douglas, Brown Shoe, and the St. Louis Cardinals, weren't buying cameras, film, and photo finishing. They were buying my dad—his energy, his knowledge, and his genuine interest in them. Somehow he knew that the most important thing a businessperson can do is to learn to see the world through the eyes of the customer.

I grew up with the lesson right in front of me, but I avoided learning it until 1994, when Bill Taylor and I were looking for a backer to put up the money to launch *Fast Company*. We were convinced that the world needed a hip new business magazine. The world was equally convinced that it already had enough business magazines, thank you very much.

The editors at *Fortune* said they couldn't see the difference between what we were proposing and what they were already doing. The people at the *Economist* said they couldn't see an audience for what we wanted to do. Every publishing house we went to told us no—until we had a meeting with Fred Drasner and Mort Zuckerman. They owned the *Atlantic Monthly* and *U.S. News & World Report*, which made them considerably smaller than the other magazine companies.

We saw that as an advantage: it meant we could get a decision from them directly, without having to fight our way through a bureaucracy.

After we'd introduced our idea to Fred and Mort we held serious discussions with Tom Evans, then the publisher of *U.S. News* and later president of the whole company. We did our best to impress Tom with the brilliance of our editorial concept, the new space we were carving out in the business magazine category. That was what we were selling—and we were selling it hard, as desperate entrepreneurs in love with their own idea are wont to do.

Tom had the decency to explain the facts of life to us. Fred and Mort weren't interested in our idea. They had a problem and we were a potential solution. Their problem was excess capacity: they had built a big pipe—ad sales staff, paper and printing contracts, relationships with advertisers, distribution contracts—and they needed another magazine to use up that excess capacity. It could be *Fast Company*, it could be *Senior Golfer*, it could be any publication that interested them and had a decent chance at succeeding.

That's when I realized that, like many entrepreneurs, I'd been looking at the situation through the wrong end of the telescope. Absorbed as I was in the brilliance of my own idea, I'd overlooked the other end of the telescope: I'd neglected to consider how the world looked to the people I was trying to sell on my idea.

When I swung the telescope around I saw the world through Fred and Mort's eyes. They needed someone to help them solve their problem. I realized that the other magazine companies had passed on *Fast Company* not because it was or wasn't a good idea but because we weren't a solution for a problem they had. Now if I wanted to sell Fred and Mort on my magazine, I first had to buy into my responsibility to help them solve their problem. I had to stop acting like an overaggressive salesman and start acting like a partner who understood and respected their side of the deal. If I could see how to solve their problem, then maybe they'd agree to solve mine.

So What?

Painters understand the difference between the object in the painting and the subject of the painting: there may be flowers in a vase on the canvas but that isn't the real subject of the painting. Moviemakers understand the difference between the plot of the film and what it's about: the story may involve a love affair interrupted by war, but the movie's really about the triumph of hope over cynicism. Even politicians get the distinction. In their campaigns they lay out policy positions on all kinds of issues, but that's not what the election is really about. In fact, the positions and the way the candidate talks about them give voters a way to evaluate the candidate's character. It's the difference between text and subtext.

But for some reason entrepreneurs and business leaders have a hard time making the distinction. Banks think they're selling loans, but customers are buying integrity; airlines think they're selling trips, but customers are buying convenience; computer companies think they're selling features, but customers are buying customer service. Starry-eyed entrepreneurs are even worse—they think the world absolutely needs their technology, their design, their next big thing.

And, as I can attest, they rarely take a look through the other end of the telescope.

If you want to get closer to your customers and see what they're buying instead of what you're selling, try this thought experiment. Take the metaphor of the telescope literally: which end are you looking through? Are you looking at your customers through your end, trying to size them up to sell them what you've got? Or are you looking back at yourself through your customers' eyes, trying to evaluate whether there might be a worthwhile solution here? What is your customer really interested in buying? What's the subtext to the customer experience, the explanation for what they're interested in? Once you've seen the world through your customers' eyes, how can you let them know that you know what they see—and that you're more than willing to provide it as part of your ongoing relationship?

Beginning to see the world through the other end of the telescope equips you to do the four things that will make the thought experiment a reality:

1. You need to talk less and listen more.

2. You need to make fewer claims and ask more questions.

3. You need to focus less on output and more on feedback.

4. You need to buy fewer ads and collect more data.

Great salespeople are commonly portrayed as great talkers. The truth is they're great listeners. They have a gift for understanding other people and a genuine interest in solving their problems. They're talented amateur psychologists. The great salesperson lets customers tell him or her what they're buying—and then builds that into the more mundane transaction that goes along with the deal.

You want to know what you're really selling? Don't tell your customers. Ask them. The journey to seeing the world through your customers' eyes begins with a single question.

KEEP TWO LISTS: WHAT GETS YOU UP IN THE MORNING? WHAT KEEPS YOU UP AT NIGHT?

Every magazine needs a tag line—the little squib that goes under the logo on the cover. But from the beginning we didn't know what to use for *Fast Company*. Finally we settled for "How smart business works" even though we knew it wasn't the perfect intuitive phrase. But at least it had *smart*, *business*, and *works* in one line.

Then about eighteen months into the life of our new magazine something unexpected happened. Business became cool. All of a sudden the new economy was front-page news. The Web was exploding. Technology was taking off. Innovation was the next big thing—every next big thing. All of a sudden America had a new attitude toward work: work didn't have to be drudgery. The work you did could make a difference, make you rich, make a dent in the universe.

I'd go to a party and people talked about . . . work. Yes, there was a new economy; but along with it there was a new conversation. People wanted to talk about where they worked. They were genuinely excited about the things going on in their workplaces. You could make up a new job title.

You could work remotely. You could be part of a team one day and generate your own assignment the next. Over and over I heard one question as the new conversation starter: "What are you working on?"

So that became our new tag line. "What are you working on?" captured the raw energy and high promise of the emerging new economy. It was as much a challenge as a question. It suggested that with all the new stuff going on you really should be working on something that got your own creative juices flowing.

That was the recognition that changed the question, at least in my own mind. It wasn't just about what people were working on. The real question was what got them out of bed in the first place. What gave them a jolt of purpose in the morning? What was waiting for them at work that got them excited? For me the powerful question that we all needed to have an answer to was "What gets you up in the morning?"

The bookend question also came from *Fast Company*. We prided ourselves on interviews with thought leaders and innovative executives—but, as with everything else in the magazine, we tried to make ours a little different. When we read interviews with CEOs in other business magazines they almost always were puff pieces; the whole point seemed to be to give the executive a platform for broadcasting the company line. So we took to opening our conversations with a counterquestion: "What keeps you up at night?" It was our way of signaling that we were playing a different game; we wanted something authentic from them. It became a *Fast Company* signature question, the way James Lipton on *Inside the Actors*

Studio can be counted on to ask his guests what they'd like to hear from St. Peter when they get to the pearly gates. Most of the time when we'd ask a CEO what kept him up at night we'd get a serious answer—because serious businesspeople relish a chance to talk about something that matters to them. Once in a while we'd get someone who'd reflexively answer, "I sleep very well at night, thank you." That one answer told us everything we needed to know about the kind of person we were dealing with.

What gets you up in the morning?

What keeps you up at night?

If you're not working on those two lists, you're wasting your precious time.

So What?

Some people just have jobs.

Others have something they really work at.

Some people are just occupied.

Others have something that preoccupies them.

It makes all the difference in the world. Think about a work life where you spend at least eight hours a day, five days a week there—or more. Think about a minimum of forty hours a week for, say, forty-seven weeks a year. Figure 1,880 hours a year. For how many years? You do the math.

What Gets You Up in the Morning? It's a tragedy of American work life. Polls vary but in general it's safe to say that more than 50 percent of American workers hate their jobs. For them, the answer to the question "What gets you up in the morning?" must be "I just need the money. I don't have a choice; I'm so numb I just do it without thinking. It doesn't really matter."

The level of energy put out by an organization's people is one of the things that separate a company you'd want to work for from one that leaks talent like a sinking boat. When I'd go visit a company I could feel it the moment I arrived. There'd be a buzz in the air created by people who are working hard and working together. Places where people know why they get up in the morning feel, sound, and move differently from places where dread and drudgery are the sum total of the work experience.

What Keeps You Up at Night? Here again America seems a troubled place. Like the statistic on Americans who hate their jobs, the data on how many Americans take sleeping pills every night are a little hard to pin down. The best estimate is at least 25 percent of Americans can't sleep at night without chemical help. It makes you wonder what keeps them up at night. Maybe it's linked to the 50 percent who hate their jobs: they can't sleep because they have nothing to get up for.

I like the question "What keeps you up at night?" because it's a chance for leaders to be honest. Much of what preoccupies men and women in positions of responsibility is of little long-term importance. Rarely do they get a chance to reflect on the things that really matter to the company's long-term viability. Business leaders who care deeply about matters of community and social change find day-to-day concerns crowding out broader issues. The things that keep leaders up at night, I've found, are the matters that never seem to find the time or place for serious engagement in the course of an ordinary workday. And, I've found, leaders genuinely believe there are things worth caring about so much, they do keep you up at night.

We all want to do work that excites us. We want to care about things that concern us.

Here's a chance to make your list so you can work on those two things.

Take out a stack of three-by-five cards. Use one to write down your answer to the question "What gets you up in the morning?" Try to keep it to one sentence. If you don't like your first answer, throw it away and do it again—it's just a three-by-five card, after all. Keep doing it until you've got an answer you can live with. When you're done with the first question, do the same exercise for the second one: "What keeps you up at night?" Work at it until you've got an honest answer.

Then read your two answers out loud to yourself. If you like them—if they give you a sense of purpose and direction—congratulations! Use them as your compass, checking from time to time to see if they're still true.

If you don't like one or both of your answers, it opens up a new question: what are you going to do about it?

Because whatever your answers are, you're spending almost two thousand hours a year of your life doing it. That makes it worthwhile to come up with answers you can not only live with but also live for.

IF YOU WANT TO CHANGE THE GAME, CHANGE THE ECONOMICS OF HOW THE GAME IS PLAYED.

Say what you will about the Grateful Dead, in my book Jerry Garcia was one smart businessperson. Here's a guitarist who was missing a piece of a finger, played in several other bands besides his own, found time to sell paintings, had a line of neckties with his name on them, and even got an ice cream flavor named after him. He also articulated a competitive strategy for the Grateful Dead that put him at the top of my list of management gurus: "You do not merely want to be considered just the best of the best. You want to be considered the only ones who do what you do."

The Grateful Dead principle of "being the only ones who do what you do" is what I decided to borrow when it came to devising *Fast Company*'s Web strategy. If you've ever been to a standard rock concert, you've heard the announcement they all make before the show: "No photography, no recording, enjoy the show."

Except for the Grateful Dead. They had a different theory of the economics, which led to a different business model, which led to a different announcement before the show:

"Tape all you want! Make all the bootlegs you want, trade them, swap them, sell them to each other."

Their fans enthusiastically complied, creating one of the earliest versions of a social network focused on live bootlegs of their favorite band. Did the band object? Not at all. Because they knew the more traffic their fans created—even if they didn't get a penny from it directly—the more tickets, T-shirts, stickers, CDs, and other Grateful Dead paraphernalia they would eventually sell. Give away the bootlegs, charge for everything else. By the way, it worked: the year Jerry Garcia died, the Grateful Dead was the highest-grossing rock-and-roll band in the United States.

Of course, Jerry Garcia wasn't the first to change the economics of his industry this way. Cyrus McCormick did it with the reaper business in the 1840s. McCormick is remembered for patenting a reaper in 1843—but that wasn't his real innovation. McCormick had quite a few competitors, but at the beginning nobody was selling any reapers, including McCormick. The problem was farmers couldn't afford the machines. So McCormick changed the economics: he invented an installment plan that let farmers buy his reaper and use the savings the machine produced to pay him back over a three-year period.

Once you start to look you'll find companies in every industry that have changed the economics to change the game: from razors to cameras, computers to airlines, magazines to nonprofits. Companies that start by redesigning the economics of an industry often finish by redesigning the whole industry—and owning it.

So What?

The game today is all about changing the game. Competing head-to-head on products and services is table stakes. Innovators are looking for a new business model that will destabilize their rivals and produce a breakthrough opportunity. In fact, in a recent survey of top-level executives in established companies IBM found that the biggest shared concern is that somewhere in the world—in a garage or a dorm room—someone is coming up with a new business model that will overthrow their established way of doing business.

How do you do it?

Start by analyzing the status quo. What's the standard economic model the industry uses today? When you pull it apart, how does it work? What are the assumptions that it's based on? How and why has it become the industry standard?

Take a look at it from the point of view of the customer. Exactly what is the customer paying for? And where does the business make its real money? Go back to Business School 101 and ask the fundamental question: what business are you really in?

After you've analyzed the standard business model, take a look outside your own industry. You may be able to learn some new tricks—or at least borrow some inspiration. What would Craigslist founder Craig Newmark do to your industry? What would happen if the whole business moved to the Web? If things that customers paid for now became free? Free, as the saying goes, is a pretty good price. What if you did a King Gillette and gave away the razor? What could you charge for? Take it one more step: are you hurting your business by charging for something you should give away free? (As daily newspapers watch their circulation numbers decline, some critics argue it would make more sense to give the papers away for free.)

After you've looked at the economics from inside the industry and from other industries, try looking at new platforms. Can you imagine new revenue streams that reflect changes going on in customer habits, customer experiences, or customer loyalty? Is emerging technology opening up new ways of connecting—or making customers pine for the good old days when things weren't so high-tech? Don't forget, everyone agreed that retail outlets were dead and all commerce was shifting to the Web. Then Steve Jobs opened up Apple stores with their Genius Bars. Counterintuitive can be a great economic model.

There are a lot of ways to reinvent an economic model. But most established companies are unwilling to do it because it would mean destabilizing their own operation.

Which is exactly what those innovators and entrepreneurs in the garages and dorm rooms are counting on.

IF YOU WANT TO CHANGE THE GAME, CHANGE CUSTOMER EXPECTATIONS.

B ack in 1970 Neil Goldschmidt was running for city council in Portland, Oregon. His campaign slogan, printed on his brochure next to his photo, said, "Neil Goldschmidt will bring city hall to you." (One astute voter who met Neil campaigning in his neighborhood took one look at the photo and the slogan and told him, "Don't bring city hall out here. We've got enough problems already.") He told voters he wanted to be in charge of city planning. When he won, the mayor, who handed out management assignments to the city commissioners, gave him the job of overseeing the city's animal shelter. Neil was in charge of dogs running at large, not city planning.

That's how I learned another important business rule transferable from the world of politics: change your customers' service expectations and you'll win their votes.

With only the responsibility for dealing with animal control, Neil had plenty of time to go out into the city's neighborhoods. Three nights a week he'd be at a different neighborhood coffee where people could tell him what they were concerned or unhappy about. Dogs running at large, it turned out, was a serious issue, particularly for older women who were afraid they'd be knocked down by a pack of dogs. Potholes came up a lot, as did traffic problems. People wanted more stop signs, speed bumps, anything to reduce traffic. Residential burglaries were a problem, as was stranger-to-stranger street crime. It was the usual array of problems that people live with on a day-to-day basis, the kinds of issues voters rarely get to talk to their elected officials about face-to-face. But here was this young, newly elected city commissioner listening to them, and also sharing some of the things he wanted to do to change the way city hall worked.

Two years later Neil was elected mayor. By then he knew more about every neighborhood in the city than anyone. He knew where every pothole was, where stop signs were needed, where there was a strong neighborhood association, and where more work was needed to help people form one. Even after becoming mayor he kept up the coffees—and he added a TV call-in show once a month where viewers could ask him questions on the air.

As mayor, he was finally able to go to work on the city planning issues he'd been concerned about in the first place. But he also created a special staff position in the mayor's office for a citizens' ombudsman: a patient and empathetic woman named Susan Kerr got the job, and we called her "the dog lady." Citizens who had a complaint or needed help dealing with the city bureaucracy went straight to her. To the people who called looking for help Susan was an effective advocate. For those of us on the mayor's staff she was a constant reminder that the whole thing had started with dogs running at large.

So What?

Whether you call them voters or subscribers, between the mayor's office and *Fast Company* I learned there were four ways to change the game by changing customer expectations.

Anticipate. As usual, Peter Drucker said it best, "One way to succeed is to work hard at not failing by always anticipating problems before they occur." If there's an example that makes the point better than any other, it was last decade's global scramble to prevent a computing meltdown with the Y2K problem. Collectively the world spent an estimated $200 billion to avert a meltdown—but the combination of anticipation and investment averted disaster.

The problem doesn't have to be of that scale to warrant your attention. It can be as simple as including batteries in the box with the electronic toy you sell, as friendly as making sure you have a prominently displayed 800 number for a customer help line. Anticipation shows your customers you're thinking about them ahead of time. It wins you points for service and, often, it can prevent an even bigger problem from developing. Remember the old saying, "The time to fix the roof is before it starts raining."

Stimulate. When Neil Goldschmidt went out to meet with voters in their living rooms he was asking for trouble. He was encouraging the people of Portland to raise their standards, lift their expectations, and put higher demands on their local elected officials. The implicit promise was that if he were elected, he'd live up to their expectations. It was a strategy with an obvious benefit and an obvious risk. The benefit was increased engagement. The risk was disappointment.

It's the same with customers today. Most of us have grown tired and disillusioned with help desks that don't help and 800 numbers that only offer automated menus. The expectation is that customer service is bad and getting worse. (Enter "bad customer service" into your favorite search engine and see what comes up.)

Now imagine the heroic response you'd get if you invited customer feedback. If you created a concierge-like service for your customers. If you hired a team of "dog ladies" to listen to the voices of your customers and become their advocates. That's the promise. Of course, there is a risk: you can't afford to overpromise and underdeliver.

Welcome. Even if you don't raise the bar by stimulating customer feedback, you can at least show that you welcome it. But that means actually making customers feel welcome, not just taking their money and taking them for granted.

There are any number of ways to make customers feel welcome, from facilitating interactions with your operation to offering shortcuts and simple solutions to common problems. If you actually listen to them, your customers will tell you how to show you care. Or learn from the best: go see how Amazon has changed the game of customer service or how Ritz-Carlton wins award after award for how it treats its customers.

The good news is that most companies are so bad, you don't have to do much to distinguish yourself from the crowd.

Most companies operate as if the CEO had adopted "let the buyer beware" as the company credo. Then they bemoan the demise of customer loyalty. They killed it and now they wonder why it's dead.

Recover. Back in 1990 when he was teaching at the Harvard Business School, Christopher Hart co-authored an *HBR* article called "The Profitable Art of Service Recovery." The premise of the article was so simple it was brilliant: every company makes mistakes, but the question is, what do you do about it? The answer was service recovery: responding quickly, genuinely, and effectively. What counts is how the customer feels after your effort at service recovery. Sometimes service recovery can serve as a shortcut to creating a closer connection with your customers because it demonstrates that you're actually capable of acting like a human. Imagine that: a company that acts human. Now that's a unique selling proposition.

THE SOFT STUFF IS THE HARD STUFF.

In the last thirty years two business books have surpassed all others in terms of popularity and impact.

The first, *In Search of Excellence*, by Tom Peters and Bob Waterman, came out in 1982. The second, *Good to Great*, by Jim Collins, came out in 2001. Twenty years separate the two books and yet they absolutely agree on one key finding: success in business is all about the quality of your people and how you treat them.

The soft stuff is the hard stuff. Period. Great people make great companies, which then leads to great financial performance. It's not the other way around.

Several years after writing *In Search of Excellence*, Tom Peters gave an interview in which he said the main purpose of his book was to overthrow "the tyranny of the bean counters"—the dominance of the finance function in corporate America. Jim Collins concluded that talent drives financial performance: who's on the bus, who's off the bus, and who sits where on the bus is ultimately more important than where the bus is going. Get the people part right and you stand a much higher chance of getting everything else right—including being able to adapt to changing circumstances you encounter along the way.

Together the two books have sold more than eight million copies. Tom and Jim are in constant demand as speakers, presenting their ideas to top management teams all over the world.

So here's the question. If business leaders are eager to read the books and hear the talks, why don't they follow the advice?

Why is finance and not human resources the most important function in the corporate cabinet? Why is it the CFO and not the VP-HR who's next in line to be CEO? If, as so many companies claim in their annual reports, "our people are our most important asset," why are people the first thing cut from the budget when the economy slows and the stock price dips? And when a company announces a massive layoff of its most valuable asset, why does the stock market reward the company with a good day of trading?

These may sound like challenging questions, but I suspect we all know the answers, even if we're uncomfortable saying them out loud.

Why do we favor finance over human resources, numbers over people? Because numbers are easy and people are hard. We can control numbers but not people. Numbers seem to obey rational laws and people are often irrational. Numbers draw from the left side of our brains, people from the right—when they're at their best, that is. We favor numbers over people because you can manipulate numbers and be perceived as a financial wizard, but if you manipulate people you're considered a mean son of a bitch.

But there's an even deeper reason for business' bias for finance over human resources. The way capitalism works in America, money is simply more important than people. Money is the default mechanism for how we keep score. The worst business leader in America will wind up on the cover of *Fortune*, *Forbes*, or *Business Week*, provided he or she is rich enough. Money equals success and success equals celebrity. In America's culture of business celebrity money isn't the root of all evil, it's the measure of all success. In contrast, leaders who try to put their people first end up being labeled soft, weak, and ineffectual. We want our leaders tough, hard, and decisive—even if it means more layoffs, and even if we know in a fundamental way it's wrong.

We know money can't buy happiness. We know Tom Peters and Jim Collins are right: in the long run the way to build up a business is by building up the people who work in the business. We know that in the long run leaders who treat their people well will outperform leaders who terrorize and exploit their people and create toxic organizations.

That's in the long run.

In the short run it's easier to go for the money.

It's what the stock market rewards. It's how organizations recognize performance. All it takes is making your numbers every quarter. In the short term it's where the payoff is because that's the way the game is rigged.

That's why Tom Peters calls it "the tyranny of the bean counters." It's a tyranny because it demands a certain kind of performance we know is wrong. Nevertheless it exerts a tyrannical hold on the way most leaders play the game.

If you want to change the game, you can't give in to the way the game is rigged. There's a choice, one of the oldest ones there is: your money or your life.

So What?

This is not an argument about whether money matters. This is an issue of personal reflection at one level and a math problem at another.

The personal issue is simple: What kind of leader do you want to be? What kind of organization do you want to run? What kind of culture do you want to create?

In issue number five of *Fast Company*, Dee Hock, the man who created VISA, boiled it all down to a test we can all take: "Who's the worst boss you ever had? Don't be like him. Who's the best boss you ever had? Be like him!"

If you can't be the kind of boss you want to be where you currently work, ask yourself why not. What values are you being asked to jettison and what values are you being asked to adopt? What are the compromises you're being asked to make? Ultimately, are you willing to be that person, to treat others that way, to have that kind of work life?

The same questions apply if you're a worker and not yet a leader. If you can't have the work life you want, what are your options? Can you carve out a small haven in your company where a different set of values can govern? One of the benefits of large companies—even those with toxic cultures—is that they are big enough to let subcultures flourish. Perhaps your part of the company can be a beachhead for change.

The other part of the exercise is a math problem. Tyrannical leaders invariably argue that economics is on their side—that their method of managing for money will produce better results, that according to the way they do the math the end does justify the means.

But Tom Peters and Jim Collins conclusively demonstrate that this equation solves the other way around: better means create better ends. Investing in people gets you a better team. A better team builds a better culture. A better culture makes for a more productive organization. That's what generates stronger, more sustainable financial results.

It doesn't work the other way around. Making tons of money doesn't produce a good workplace, a healthy culture, or even happy, motivated people. This math problem works only if you start with the people and work it through to the financial results.

You don't have to take my word for it.

Read *In Search of Excellence* and *Good to Great*.

If you've already read them, read them again. They're that excellent. And great.

IF YOU WANT TO BE LIKE GOOGLE, LEARN MEGAN SMITH'S THREE RULES.

In the center of SY Partners' office in San Francisco stands the Innovation Lab. The design of the space itself, with its glass walls and sleek work spaces, suggests that hip, cool, creative stuff goes on in there. It's the kind of place you can easily imagine spawning innovation. It's the kind of place you hope to be invited to so you can experience innovation.

For two days in June 2006 this high-powered space was the scene of an experimental gathering convened by the Japan Society of New York: Connecting Communities, a meeting of the Innovators Network, a loose configuration of business, cultural, and social leaders from Japan and the United States. The purpose of the gathering was to focus on intersections between community and innovation—to spark new conversations, better understandings, and closer collaboration between the widely divergent traditions and cultures of the two countries.

I was there to act as one of the moderators—which meant my job was to listen carefully and attentively to everything anybody said. In a group electric with spontaneous creativity, I knew the most offhand comment could translate into a memorable lesson.

Which was how I happened to be paying careful attention when Megan Smith, Google's director of new business development and strategy, almost casually let slip her three little rules—rules that I instantly stapled like headlines to my forehead.

When you say "Google" it makes you listen more attentively. Add in Megan's job title and you're almost obliged to stand at attention. Which is not at all an accurate portrayal of Megan Smith. What's most impressive about her is everything else she's done besides Google: she earned a degree in mechanical engineering from MIT, worked at one of the early mobile computing companies, and served as CEO at a dynamic Web site for the gay and lesbian community. Her work at Google is just her day job; she's also a Reuters Digital Fellow at Stanford and an advisor to Design That Matters, an organization that connects problems in the Third World with young engineering students who want to contribute their technical expertise. At this event, as I watched and listened, I noticed that Megan often stood off to one side, and that when she did speak it was usually quietly. She wasn't trying to be a big shot with a big shot's job title. She was trying to share what she knew from her experience for the benefit of everyone there.

So what were Megan's rules? (For the record, she didn't call them rules, but that's how they instantly struck me and why I immediately wrote them down.)

Megan Smith's Three Rules

1. The customer participates.

2. The customer drives.

3. Open systems beat closed systems.

Now you know them too.

Lots of good things were said in that glass-walled room. There were plenty of insights about business, social change, and the intersection of the two. But Megan's rules stood out. They're how we all need to be in business starting yesterday. If you're one of the smart ones who's already doing what Megan described, good for you. You're in the game, if not ahead of it. But if you're not already practicing these three rules, you need to ask yourself why not. And then you need to get started. Now.

Because chances are somewhere out there is a competitor who does know Megan's rules and is already applying them. That means you're in trouble.

So What?

Every leader I've ever met, from politics to business, shares one overriding attribute: they're all control freaks. They all think they're in control. Which is undoubtedly the biggest illusion of our time. Anyone who thinks they are in control of anything needs to check into the twelve-step program of his or her choice. Any CEO who thinks she's in control of her company needs to sit down and watch a full season of *The Office*. And any elected official who thinks he's in control of his career or his jurisdiction needs to attend a screening of *All the President's Men*.

Because the unstated fourth proposition of Megan's rules is "You are not in control." Who is? Now we're getting somewhere!

The Customer Participates. It doesn't matter what business you're in or what work you do. The line between producer and consumer is blurring. Doctors used to be gods, patients supplicants. Now patients show up in their doctors' offices armed with their own diagnoses and extensive printouts from the Web. Whether professional reporters like it or not, bloggers are journalists. Even the most clueless ad agency has discovered the seduction of a contest that lets consumers make their own ads: customers are their own marketers.

The Customer Drives. Comfortable with the idea that the customer is sitting in the car with you? Good! Now it's time to up the ante. Move over—that's the customer sitting in the driver's seat. You're a passenger in your own car.

In an information economy what seems a mobility-navigational metaphor is more than a metaphor. Customers do drive around the Web looking for sites that entertain or inform them. With satellite radio and a choice of dish or cable equipped with TiVo, listeners and viewers can drive around those dials as well, skipping ads, recording what they want, and making a date with themselves to enjoy their choices whenever they want. Customers aren't fickle; they're just doing the driving.

Your job? Your job is to learn to accept the fact that you're not driving anymore. Your job is to provide the entertainment for the driver. The more you relax, the more your customer will relax—and you do want a relaxed driver, don't you? Much better for business than an uptight driver stuck in a nasty traffic jam. So what you're in charge of is creating the most exceptional, enjoyable customer experience you can conceive of. You're another roadside attraction. That's it.

Open Systems Beat Closed Systems. Business examples abound. But one example trumps all the rest: the fall of the Soviet Union. Some give credit to Ronald Reagan; others cite the Pope's influence. I maintain it was the power of open systems and the hopelessness of closed systems—especially in a global information economy. If America's manufacturing might was the arsenal of democracy in World War II, our open system model is the network of democracy in the competition for the future.

If your company is still a closed system, here's your choice: do you want to play the role of Konstantin Chernenko or Mikhail Gorbachev? If you want to be on the right side of history, you'll embrace open systems. They save money, increase speed, invite participation, require flexibility, and thrive on democracy. They break down barriers, promote pragmatism, spotlight talent, and reward real performance. Open systems beat closed systems. It's a race to the future. Whoever gets there first wins.

"Denmark has high wages, high taxes, and an expensive social safety net," I said. "But your manufacturing is moving to cheaper countries. What's the strategy for the future?"

"We're not worried," she said. "We intend to compete on the quality of our design. Denmark is famous for our design."

I think you can see where this is heading.

I got the same answer in Florence, in São Paulo, and in Stockholm. In Toronto they were proud of the quality of their urban design. In the Dongtan planned city in Shanghai, China, they're designing an eco-friendly city from scratch. Singapore is redesigning the entire country, from its education system to its cybereconomy.

Today design is differentiation. Companies use design to create distinctive products and services that capture their customers' imaginations; to restructure their corporate operations; to unveil new logos and uniforms that express a fresh corporate identity; to develop new communications tools that connect with customers and shareholders; to build corporate offices that encourage and enable collaboration; to collect and share information across a global platform. Design is a way to solve deep-seated social problems. And design is a money saver, a way to simplify products and make them easier and less expensive to manufacture.

It wasn't always like this. In the old days, designers were the people at the end of the production process. Engineers handed them something they'd developed and told designers to "pretty it up." Those days are officially over.

GOOD DESIGN IS TABLE STAKES.
GREAT DESIGN WINS.

In the last few years since I left *Fast Company* and started traveling a lot, I've noticed a global leitmotif, as if the same piece of music were being played in different countries all over the world.

In Tokyo at a conference on innovation I sat down with an old friend, a business sociologist and strategist for leading Japanese companies.

"Japan used to be a low-cost exporter of manufactured goods," I said. "But those days are clearly over. What's Japan's new national strategy?"

"We don't think there's a problem," she told me. "Japan intends to compete globally on the quality of our design."

It made sense to me. Japan has an exquisite sense of style and presentation.

Not long after that trip I went to Denmark for a conference that brought together architects, industrial designers, and graphic artists. I walked around Copenhagen, admiring the shops and stores, the comfortable restaurants, the overall ambience of the place. Then I had a cup of coffee with a friend who had organized the gathering.

Today "starchitects" such as Frank Gehry are sought after by governments from China to Dubai to do for them what he did for Bilbao. The designs of J Mays at Ford and Chris Bangle at BMW have created camps of followers and spawned hordes of imitators, as has Jonathan Ive for his designs at Apple. Tinker Hatfield at Nike originally trained as an architect before turning to shoes. David Kelley, founder and chairman of IDEO, gets credit for spearheading the "D" school at Stanford, a cross-disciplinary program to combine smart business practices with cutting-edge design skills. Across the board designers have defined a way of seeing that adds to the delight of customers and the profitability of companies.

When it comes to the role of design in business, the old days are gone. The war is over.

Design won.

So What?

My guess is that most of you already get it. You already know that the design of your Web site says more about your brand than any thirty-second TV spot. You know that little—and not so little—things such as the design of your logo and letterhead, the design of your business card, and your office space all communicate instantly what your operation is all about, whether you're a company of one or one hundred thousand.

But perhaps design is still a mystery to you. You know it's important but can't quite find a way into its language, specs, and tricks. Here are three ways for you to start to crack the design code.

Reading. If you're a word person trying to learn about seeing, there are any number of terrific books that will get you started. Begin with Dan Pink's *A Whole New Mind*. It's entertaining and instructive; you'll discover that you're probably a left-brained business thinker in an increasingly right-brained economy. Once you accept that new fact of life you can use Dan's exercises and extensive reading list to delve deeper into the world of design. Anything by Tom Kelley of IDEO will expand your appreciation of design and innovation; Don Norman's classic *The Design of Everyday Things* will help you see the world with fresh eyes. If you want to see the world through green eyes, read Will McDonough's *Cradle to Cradle*.

Viewing. According to Dan Pink, medical schools in the United States have started taking their students to art museums. The point isn't to turn them into art collectors. It's to have them practice seeing—a critical skill for aspiring diagnosticians. For aspiring entrepreneurs or business leaders the same skill is vital and the same practice can help. The more you look at art the more you develop your appreciation for how design works. If museums and galleries don't do it for you, try furniture and interior design. It's worth spending an afternoon looking at rugs, fabrics, and furniture to see what you like and don't like, what you consider graceful, and what appears awkward. Or if you can't imagine an afternoon of carpets but you love cars, make a design field trip to your favorite dealerships. Don't worry about price; you're not buying. But look carefully at the lines, interior detailing, and small amenities that give each car its own performance. As Yogi Berra once said, "You can observe a lot just by watching."

Shopping. No, not for the car. But go out and buy an assortment of smaller objects you can put in your home and office. Go to your nearest kitchen store and pick out a variety of OXO products, from a peeler to a teakettle. If you hold any of these items in your hand, you'll immediately understand what "consumer-centered design" means. If you don't already have one, order an Aeron chair. There's a reason it's in the Museum of Modern Art in New York. Go to the nearest Bang & Olufsen showroom and pick out a phone or a TV, depending on your budget. Need a new laptop? Stop by an Apple store and purchase a new MacBook Air. Critics say it's underpowered and overpriced. But it's also flat, light, and gorgeous. Feel free to add your own favorites to the shopping list. Go to the part of your city where the antique stores are and see what great design looked like in the past. Or if you prefer virtual shopping, check out the Web for design-centered sites.

When you're done with your shopping spree, assemble all the items you've bought in your office or home and take a look. When it comes to line, color, shape, size, material, functionality, what do these products have in common? Are they as good to look at as they are fun to use? Is there an emotional content to their design? Is there a distinctive "cool factor" that comes from the design?

Then, after you've taken a careful account of the ways they

look, feel, and perform, check one other thing: price. That's something else they all have in common. Great design lets you charge more.

All that shopping too expensive for you? No problem: treat it as a field trip. You don't have to buy a thing to get the idea. But you do need to buy into the idea: design is everywhere, and increasingly design is everything.

WORDS MATTER.

Aarhus, Denmark, is famous for two things: its café society, which rivals the best in the world, and the KaosPilots, its school for social entrepreneurs that is the best for the world. But that's getting ahead of the story.

I was introduced to the KaosPilots and its founder, Uffe Elbaek, in 1994, before "social entrepreneurs" had become a familiar phrase. (It is an interesting juxtaposition: *social* and *entrepreneurs*. It was striking back in 1994 but today it's a growing field for people who want to produce social change using smart business models.) Uffe originally pioneered the KaosPilots to help young students who didn't fit into traditional job categories. With Uffe's leadership it has evolved into a unique educational blend emphasizing real-world project management skills, systems thinking, and collaborative problem solving.

Despite being both tiny and different from most Danish schools (or perhaps because of it), the KaosPilots took off, and Uffe, quite proudly, began to promote it as "the best school in the world." The boast was partly tongue-in-cheek, because most of the world had never heard of the KaosPilots. Still, it was true that the KaosPilots' commitment to making a difference in the world entitled Uffe to do a little bragging.

Then Uffe started listening to his own words and he had a better idea.

There were plenty of schools that liked to claim they were the "best in the world." Every college and university tried to stake its claim to that title. But for the KaosPilots it was a boast that didn't fit—it didn't describe the school's philosophy, its purpose, or its relationship to the world. Uffe realized that the KaosPilots exist not to be the best in the world but to save the world.

So he changed the KaosPilots' slogan. It became "the best school *for* the world."

The difference comes down to one little preposition, used in the right place in the right way. But it makes all the difference in the world.

So What?

1. "The difference between the right word and the almost-right word is the difference between lightning and the lightning bug." Mark Twain said that.

2. "If you think learning your vocabulary words doesn't make a difference, try going into a store and asking for toilet paper when you only know the word for sandpaper." Roy Battenberg, my high school German teacher, said that.

3. If you aren't convinced that words matter, consider the backstory to the recent global financial meltdown that originated with preposterous lending practices— practices that turned out to cost tens of thousands of people their homes and the world several years of economic turmoil. A front-page *New York Times* story explained how banks manipulated the English language to scam unsuspecting borrowers. The punch line: banks changed the words from "second mortgage" to "equity access," tricking borrowers into thinking they were doing something with their homes that, in the words of one banker, "sounds more innocent."

What sounded "more innocent" became the cause of a historic global economic disaster. At that point, in an Orwellian twist, innocent becomes guilty.

4. You don't know what you think until you write it down. As an editor, I've heard a lot of sloppy pitches offered as important ideas from very smart people. My advice is always the same: write it down. That's the only way to know what you're trying to say. When you look at the words you see what you're thinking. You don't need to be a "writer" to be a good writer. But we all do need to write, and it counts if you write well. Whether it's a simple thank-you letter, a memo, a slide deck, or a speech in front of the whole company, write it down. Look at the words. Do they make sense? Do they say what you're trying to say? Are they the right words—or

close to the right words? The right words make all the difference.

5. Here are a few things to think about when you sit down to write. Make an outline. Sketch out the direction of your argument in advance; you can use three-by-five cards to organize your thoughts. Unless you are Tom Wolfe and have your own distinctive writing style, there's a lot to be said for short sentences and active verbs. Punchy is good. Avoid the passive voice, and, as my fifth-grade English teacher, Russ Bissell, taught me, you are to never split an infinitive. When in doubt cut it out. We had a rule at *Fast Company*: you can cut any article by one-third without doing harm. When you use jargon you don't seem smarter—you're just harder to understand. Business leaders who can write good, plain English and explain their ideas without using endless streams of acronyms will get much better results. They also avoid having their audiences play buzzword bingo while they're speaking.

THE LIKELIEST SOURCES OF GREAT IDEAS ARE IN THE MOST UNLIKELY PLACES.

Where do great ideas come from?

For a while big companies thought they had the answer: R&D labs. Hire the best brains. Let them work on important problems. Win Nobel Prizes. Produce big breakthroughs. Rinse. Repeat.

Then 3M came up with the Post-it note and corporate America fell in love with the idea of innovation in your spare time. Shut down those expensive R&D labs and let your employees use 10 percent or 15 percent of their time to fool around on their own projects. Maybe there were untapped Post-it notes sitting at all those desks.

That was good for a while, until corporate leaders began to notice innovative start-ups. In every industry there were these pesky little boutique outfits that insisted on doing things differently. Where were these guys coming up with all their great ideas? Pouring salt into the corporate wounds, one innovation analyst estimated that small entrepreneurs accounted for 95 percent of all radical innovations in the United States since World War II.

That's when it got smart for big companies to partner with or even acquire some of these start-ups. Procter & Gamble declared that the not-invented-here syndrome was responsible for not-invented-much results and said it was going to supplant R&D with C&D: connect and develop. Fifty percent of the company's new ideas would come from outside its corporate walls. IBM confirmed the practice with a survey: 765 CEOs said they got most of their ideas from outside their own companies.

So where *do* great ideas come from?

From the Trenches. The best example of trench-based innovation I ever heard came from John Seely Brown when he was running Xerox's Palo Alto Research Center.

The way JSB tells the story, Xerox, faced with an economic downturn, was ready to lay off a bunch of its tech reps—the guys who drove around in trucks fixing broken Xerox machines. The company knew it had too many of them because they always seemed to have time to stop and have coffee between service calls. But before the company pulled the trigger on the tech reps, it got in touch with JSB and asked his advice: did it make sense to lay these guys off?

JSB came back with his answer: "First let's hire some anthropologists." That's right, anthropologists, who would ride around with the tech reps and see what they actually do.

What did they find? That the tech reps were bona fide knowledge workers. They didn't follow the company repair manuals—they used them to prop open the doors of the trucks. Instead they invented work-arounds to the problems they found in the field, then, over coffee, they shared their best practices. They were technical innovators.

Instead of laying off the tech reps Xerox invested in communications technology so they could more easily talk to each other—and the company could capture what it heard. The result: design solutions to problems that had plagued the machines for years.

Where did the great ideas come from? The guys with the dirty fingernails, working in the trenches.

From Customers, Suppliers, and Competitors. Ever since Sony cofounder Akio Morita said that customers never would have come up with the Sony Walkman because they don't know how to ask for what doesn't yet exist, looking to customers for ideas has gotten a bad rap. But now another innovative Japanese entrepreneur is out to prove Morita-san wrong.

Kohei Nishiyama has created a Web site called Cuusoo, which roughly translates as "wish" or "imaginary." Customers can post their wishes on the site or they can survey the site and put in their orders for wishes that others have put there. When enough customers have ordered an item, Kohei fulfills their wish: he builds and delivers what they've already ordered. Kohei's model, called "design to build," is his great idea; the orders placed by his customers are their great ideas. Together it's an example of collaborative innovation.

From Pissed-off Employees. Wouldn't it be great if happy, motivated workers always came up with great ideas? Well, instead sometimes it's the ones who are alienated and have something to prove. Kenichi Ohmae, Japan's most prolific strategist and celebrated management writer, told me the story of two workers in one of Japan's large consumer electronic companies who were rotated from good jobs to an assignment they both considered demeaning: the small kitchen appliance division. Filled with anger, the two men determined to show their bosses what a stupid decision they'd made. To exact their revenge they turned to the humblest kitchen appliance they could think of: the coffeemaker.

They started with a question: what does it take to make a great cup of coffee? They listed the variables: water (temperature, quality, and quantity), beans (freshness, quality, and grind), filter (material, quality, and cleanliness), and carafe (material, quality, and temperature). It took one year to get answers and most of another to build and test a prototype. When they were done they'd designed and built a completely new home coffeemaker. The machine, the system, the components—all were the result of new thinking. They not only revitalized the coffeemaker business, they also perked up the whole home appliance line.

And they earned a well-deserved promotion.

From the Periphery. It used to be that the farther away from headquarters you worked the lower your chances of making it to the top. Then along came globalization. There was cool stuff going on far from home. Some of that cool stuff turned into major innovations. Levi Strauss & Co., headquartered in San Francisco and deeply committed to denim, found a phenomenon in Japan: a relaxed-look, relaxed-fit style of pants that didn't even use denim. When Dockers came to the United States it was just in time for casual Fridays. It triggered a new thought about innovation: there were all kinds of great ideas "out there" waiting to be brought back "in here." Hospitals have started looking at cockpit checklist practices to cut down on operating room mistakes. Professional football teams have borrowed technology from YouTube and social networks to streamline their analyses of game film. Western pharmaceutical companies are exploring native cures and medicines developed from obscure jungle plants. U.S. television executives are importing British programming to find new hits. Not only are great ideas "out there," so is the future.

So What?

Innovation is the coin of the realm. It dominates the business conversation. Plug the word into your favorite search engine and you'll be rewarded with more than 150 million items. Let me see if I can boil it down to just four.

First, innovation is a verb, not a noun. The venues listed above all have one thing in common: they all require active listening, scanning, learning, adapting—all kinds of verbs—on the part of would-be innovators. Knowing where to look for great ideas is part of the solution. But knowing how to look and how to listen is even more important.

Innovation comes from a willingness to go, look, and listen—to open up your mind, see with fresh eyes, and practice active listening. If you want to be an innovator, you have to work like one, think like one, listen like one, ask questions like one, learn like one. Innovation isn't a thing; it's a way of being.

Second, innovation happens from a combination of applied effort—at the Edison Labs perspiration outscored inspiration 99 percent to 1 percent—and from applied relaxation. There's no doubt that great ideas come from hard work and routinized effort. Companies that want to make innovation a way of doing business turn it into a measurable, predictable program. At the same time, new research on the brain shows that people have remarkable moments of insight most often when they stop trying to have remarkable moments of insight. The way to approach great ideas is the way you look at the sun: you look, and then you look away.

Third, like money, not all great ideas are created equal. Like children, if they're yours, you may love them all equally. But unlike your children, you're allowed to rank your ideas by their feasibility, likelihood of success, return on investment, and other market-based measures. It's fun to come up with great ideas; implementing them is hard work. Use your discretion.

Fourth, great ideas really are the coin of the realm—if you can implement them. Otherwise they're fool's gold. Most companies have people who are nothing but idea people and others who are only implementers. You need them both. Great idea people are rare—and also frequently hard to live with. They see things the rest of us can't see, which is their gift. They can't see what you and I can see easily, which is their burden. Still, you need them and they need a home where they can contribute. Treat them differently from the rest of us, make them feel welcome, and explain them to your implementers, who may have a hard time appreciating them. Your job is to build a bridge the great ideas can walk across, from those who have them to those who make them real.

If you can create an organization with that culture, you'll have the best of both worlds. And you'll have found the best place of all to look for great ideas: your own.

EVERYTHING COMMUNICATES.

If a college student who's studying business communications wears a do-rag to class, is it a problem?

That was the question handed me when I reported to Baruch College in New York to give a talk on business and communications to an audience of professors of business communications.

Here's what I said: If everything you say and do communicates, then the way a student dresses sends an unmistakable message. Wearing a do-rag is a conscious choice. You can't call it an accident or an inadvertent style statement. If a student shows up to a class on business communications wearing a do-rag, I'd say he's practicing the art of communication. Whether he deserves extra credit for taking the class to heart is a different question—but this student has already learned how to send messages.

Is it a problem? Well, that depends. If he goes looking for a job with his do-rag and his aim is to get hired at a hip new ad agency that's selling itself as a collection of cool hunters, a do-rag could be a way of displaying his own street cred (or at least it could back when this took place). If he wears it every day and everywhere he goes, it could be a personal branding item, like Steve Jobs' blue jeans and black turtlenecks or Malcolm Gladwell's mop of hair. On the other hand, if he wears it to a traditional company that has strict ideas about dress codes and personal grooming—say, a uniform of dark suits, white shirts, and dark ties—a do-rag could definitely present a problem, assuming he wanted a job in that kind of place to begin with.

But like all clear communications, wearing or not wearing a do-rag is really just a footnote (or headnote). It matters less whether you wear a do-rag and more whether you know who you are in the first place. It's hard to communicate who you are and what you stand for if you don't know yourself. Once you know who you are, how you say it gets a lot easier.

So What?

"Everything communicates" is the fundamental message of Tom Peters' *Fast Company* classic, "The Brand Called You." Companies, products, and services aren't the only things that get branded; we are all brands. In an economy of knowledge workers and free agents, project-based employment and team-based activities, we have to decide what our brand stands for. We have to identify our brand values and then live them and express them. And that may include wearing a do-rag. Or not.

What does your brand stand for? Are you the person whose brand is all about old-fashioned hard work and unlimited effort—the workhorse of the organization? Or are you the person whose brand is all about creativity—the idea guy in the organization? The person who can be counted on to show up on time every time, or the person who'll dash in at the last second with a brilliant insight? The person who will speak the truth under even the most difficult circumstances, or the person who will make peace between warring factions?

Each of us is a brand, and every choice we make communicates what our brand stands for.

Your business card communicates, from the shape and size to the choice of title and font. If it's vertical and thin, it says you're Web-savvy and downloaded free software to make your own cards. If it has Japanese on the back, it says you travel to Japan a lot and you respect their practices. If you go to a meeting and you don't bring a card, well, that sends a message too.

Your personal practices communicate. One of Tom Peters' habits is always to write thank-you notes. When a person as busy as Tom takes the time to drop you a handwritten thank-you note after a meeting, it tells you something about the kind of person he is. Small gestures send big signals. (For instance, if you're a large American car company and you're appealing to Congress for an emergency loan to keep your business afloat, flying to Washington, D.C., in your private jet is probably not sending the right message.)

Your Web site communicates. Because design is so immediate, Web sites offer direct clues to the culture of a company. I've spent hours decoding the Web sites of law firms, consulting firms, and other personal services businesses. It's often the case that the claims made in writing on the site are directly contradicted by the way it performs—without the firm knowing it. It's not just how the site looks; it's how it welcomes its visitors, how it's organized, how easy it is to navigate.

Your office communicates—all the way down to the furniture. When I worked at *HBR* and again at *Fast Company* I made sure I had a round table in my office. I wanted meetings to be roundtable conversations, not boardroom sessions with me sitting in the seat of power. But it's not just your own office that sends a signal; it's the building you work in. There's a reason banks were all built of marble in the days before the FDIC: marble said "security." When Steelcase built its corporate pyramid and distributed coffee bars throughout the office space, it was sending a message to its employees: "Go ahead! Hang out at the coffee bar—you'll probably come up with some good ideas that way." The company was telling its people it wanted creative offices for them, just like the ones they designed for their customers.

How you communicate *communicates*. Some people think they need to "speak business" to prove they belong in business. They think a compulsive use of consulting buzzwords and MBA jargon makes them sound like they've learned the secret code. Unfortunately, that kind of acronym-laced talk doesn't demonstrate a business-smart brand; it comes across as "the brand called insecure." A far better strategy is to know all the right jargon but to translate it into words and ideas that ordinary people can understand. Your brand is a lot more valuable if you can talk business using real English. How about the message you use on your e-mail when you're going to be away? The way you word that message sends, well, a message. The same goes for the recording you use for voice mail. My favorite was the one my son, Adam, used: "Leave your beep after my message." He's very funny, very creative, and dyslexic—all of which is in his message.

And yes, your way of dressing communicates, from the tip of your Crocs to the top of your do-rag.

So first figure out what your brand is. Then remember that everything you do—and don't do—communicates it.

CONTENT ISN'T KING.
CONTEXT IS KING.

B ack in the 1990s Web-preneurs had a mantra: "Content is king." At the time it made sense—or at least it provided a metaphor for making sense out of so much change. The idea was that building the Web was like laying pipes. It was comforting to think of IT spending as infrastructure investment and not just huge sums of money being spent on pure faith. Once the pipes were laid, the business logic went, those who had the most stuff to push through the pipes would make the most money. In other words, content was king.

I thought they were wrong.

I thought context was king. Context was why an article in *HBR* carried more authority than one in a commercial business magazine. Context was why Fortune 500 companies paid more for advice from McKinsey than from a new, untested consulting firm. Information is a commodity. Context creates value.

Information may want to be free, but it isn't neutral. That was the lesson taught by Norman Mailer, Jimmy Breslin, and the New Journalism of the 1960s. Objectivity is a convention, and an illogical one at that. Journalists can have rules to guide them: how many sources it takes to confirm a fact, what constitutes on and off the record, how to fact-check a story, why it's important to check out the other side of the story. But that's only a patina of objectivity lightly covering the deep decisions that guide reporting. What do you leave in and what do you leave out? What's at the top of the story and what's at the end? What adjectives and adverbs do you employ to modify the neutral facts that make up the story? And the most basic question: what qualifies as news?

But it's not just the news business. It's all business.

I was working on an *HBR* piece with Citibank's legendary Walter Wriston in his New York office when he gave me a short course on content versus context.

"Every day I'm presented with three types of information," Wriston said. "Facts, wrong facts, and damned lies. My job is to know which is which."

In other words, his job was to assert the value of context over content.

But he also had a larger message. In business what we value most is a trusted point of view. That's what Wriston was paying his top people for; it's what the best bosses everywhere want from their value-adding employees: evaluation, interpretation, analysis, synthesis, perspective, judgment—context.

Information is cheap. It's bland. It lacks texture, energy, purpose, meaning, or value.

What we're all looking for from others—and what we should hone as our own capability—is a convincing, compelling vision of how the world works.

What's valuable is having your own point of view and having the confidence to express it. Anything else is available 24/7 on the Web and everywhere else—which makes it worthless.

So What?

No one knows more about context than entrepreneurs and artists. I saw Isabel Allende bring a whole new context to a discussion of the meaning of legacy at the Waldzell conference in September 2007.

I had moderated a morning panel discussion with representatives of the world's greatest religions, from a leading rabbi from Jerusalem to the Dalai Lama, wise men all.

In the afternoon, Isabel took the stage with a surge of energy.

"I think *legacy* is a very patriarchal word," she said. Everyone in the room sat up a little straighter. "Fifty-one percent of the population are women and most religious leaders are male. The idea of legacy has a different meaning for women than for men. I have one experience that 51 percent of humanity has had—the experience of boundless, unconditional love. I am talking about the moment of childbirth. If women could bring that to the table of the world, that would be our wonderful legacy."

That's an artist talking. In a fifteen-minute talk she added a completely new and powerful context to a traditional discussion of legacy. She talked about something she knew deeply—and because she shared her feelings, she endowed us with a new context.

Context is how we all add value. But how do you develop

the practice to know what you know, to see how you see the world?

The answer is that context comes to those who develop their way of seeing and making sense of the world. It comes to those who build their confidence and competence for expressing it. That's why artists and entrepreneurs thrive: they work at how they see the world and they practice expressing it through their works of innovation or their works of art. Like anything else, context only comes with practice.

If you don't watch the news regularly and get into a shouting match with your TV set, you're not practicing. They're not telling you the news; they're telling you how they see the news. You're entitled to tell them back.

If you don't check multiple Web sites for news and analysis daily and register your profound disagreement with their takes on the events of the day, you're not developing your own context. Your job is to use their reports as a whetstone to sharpen your own analyses.

If you don't clip one or more newspapers—either the paper or electronic versions—and then work at assembling the clips into your own take on how the world works, you're not building your mental muscles. The point of the exercise is to collect the dots so you can connect the dots.

If you don't go out with your friends from work, school, church, or sports and argue vigorously about books, ideas, the economy, the next election, or the trajectory of the technological revolution, you're never going to develop your own compelling perspective. It takes practice.

A few years ago economist Robert Reich wrote that we were destined to become a nation of "symbolic analysts," people who make a living by manipulating ideas to find innovative solutions to difficult problems. Another term might be "context creators": people who connect the dots in ways that make sense, provide insight, deliver meaning, and produce ways of seeing the world that lead to new solutions that work.

This skill, this capacity to create context, is a valuable asset to you and your company. It's the first job of an engaged citizen—to think and make sense of the events that shape our country and the world. It's the best job in any company—to provide insight and independent thinking.

No matter how many raw facts you know, they're only as valuable as the context within which you put them. That's why context is more important than content and always will be, pipes or no pipes.

EVERYTHING IS A PERFORMANCE.

This rule may come as something as a surprise to you, given the number of times I've sung the anthem of authenticity and hummed a chorus or two of "all knowledge begins with self-knowledge."

All of that's true; none of that contradicts the notion that you've got to have an act. In politics, business, art, public speaking, even in putting out a magazine, you've got to have an act.

Fast Company had an act, as did *HBR*. *HBR*'s act was "Anything this hard to read has to be important." And, by extension, if you had it on your credenza, whether you'd read it or not, you were important. After I left *HBR* to start *Fast Company*, I used to say that *HBR* was a bran muffin: it was good for you, but it was awfully hard to swallow. *Fast Company* was designed to be a blueberry muffin. Our act was to be graphically fun and visually playful, to make our articles fast-paced and our language colorful. We wanted readers to get a serious business education without really knowing it. We called our act "edu-tainment."

To work on our act we looked at others we admired. For example, we compared each issue of *Fast Company* to a great rock album. Like the best albums (Bill Taylor thought of Bruce Springsteen's greatest hits; I imagined Bob Dylan's), each issue of the magazine needed a hard rocking number, a love song, a tune that could make it to the top of the charts, a sad song, a slow song, and maybe something personal and reflective. It wasn't hard to map the components of an album to the architecture of a magazine: the front of the book was an opener that got things off to a good start, the chart buster was our cover story, a love song was an in-depth profile, a slow bluesy tune was a reflective story of business or personal adversity, and then something fast and upbeat left the reader in a good mood at the end. A magazine, like an album, was a collection of small performances that came together to produce a coherent act. Each piece had a different rhythm or pacing, but all the pieces came from a single, unified persona. The magazine had a voice.

Great singers, actors, politicians give great performances. CEOs who recognize their roles as leaders know that every time they appear in public or in front of their employees they are under a microscope—or in front of a spotlight that casts a larger-than-life shadow. Every gesture is a part of a performance. The question is, do you know you have an act—and do you know what it is?

So What?

I learned about having an act when *Fast Company* became a hit and Bill and I started getting requests to appear on business-oriented TV shows. It seemed like a good idea to do some "media training" to prepare, even though I thought my experience in politics had taught me how to answer—or not to answer—a tough question. The media training consisted of a trained professional asking me questions, videotaping my answers, and showing them to me. That's when I got to see why I needed an act—or more accurately, how bad my act was.

I did get to see how I came across. I was going for sincerity, for aw-shucks modesty. What I saw came across as painful self-consciousness. But it wasn't in what I said. It was largely things I wasn't even aware of. Hand motions, body language, little facial tics—not attractive! I saw myself on videotape doing things I'd been totally unaware of only minutes before. When I could see them, I could fix them.

I got a second lesson in the importance of having an act when a friend told me one of his experiences as an executive coach working with a CEO who had a notoriously bad reputation. His direct reports didn't like working for him. He had alienated his board. His job was on the line—which was why he hired my friend to shadow him and tell him what he saw as a way of coaching him.

The problem, my friend quickly observed, wasn't that the CEO made bad decisions. In the privacy of his own office he was fine. But when he got into a public arena he lost it. He didn't know it, he couldn't see it, but in public he was so uncomfortable in his own skin he made everyone around him uncomfortable. He didn't seem to trust himself, so others felt they couldn't trust him either. Holding up a mirror to his act—or his two acts, one private, one public—helped him see how he was undermining his effectiveness and his career.

How do you develop an act? What are some of the building blocks you can work on?

Conviction, for one thing. If people feel you genuinely

care—about the work you're doing, about them, or about the theme of the talk you're giving—they are much more willing to enter into your performance with you. You connect with them, they connect with you. That's one reason question-and-answer sessions are often much more energetic than the long speeches that precede them: Q&A turns a monolog into a dialog.

Mastery of the material is an important piece. It doesn't matter if you're delivering a sales presentation with PowerPoint or a rock concert with an electric guitar. If you can handle your chosen instrument like a pro, you carry your audience along with you.

Consistency, coherence, and consideration are essential too. It's hard to follow a performer who's constantly changing his act, altering his accent, shifting his stance (unless it's either Bob Dylan or Pablo Picasso). As an audience, we want to know something about who a performer is, what he or she is trying to get across, and whether we can trust that person to deliver. That's true of all performers, including business leaders.

One thing this doesn't mean: you don't need to be a twenty-four-karat phony. You don't need to learn to pretend to be someone you're not. Quite the opposite. The best act a person can mount is an amplification of his or her most essential self. It's as if you'd taken a spotlight, placed it in front of you, and used it to cast an even larger image of yourself for others to see you more clearly. It makes you bolder, brighter, and more intense. The goal is to make yourself so comfortable with your skills and your public self that you have no fear of projecting yourself onto a bigger stage. Not a different you, just a bigger you.

SIMPLICITY IS THE NEW CURRENCY.

I was standing in a Chinese-themed bar in San Francisco surrounded by more than a hundred Web-savvy social entrepreneurs. What had been billed as a networking opportunity actually resembled a hundred hummingbirds exchanging business cards and proselytizing on behalf of their new change-the-world Web applications.

Over the din a couple of young friends of mine were shouting about a new development.

"Have you heard about the new Web browser that's launching?" she asked. "It's just for social entrepreneurs."

"What's it do?" he asked.

"It becomes your default browser," she said. "Everything that comes up is about social entrepreneurship. Plus it has a social networking element, all bundled together."

"I wonder if it would make life easier or more complicated," he said. "Would I use it or would it just get in the way?"

Exactly!

It was iPod-like music to my ears to hear these two young techno-activists acknowledge the central contradiction of the last twenty years: our technology has crossed the line from solution to burden.

Most of us feel our human capacities taxed to the max every day. We have more of everything except time. Marshall McLuhan said it: "First we shape our tools and then they shape us." What we're learning is that being shaped by our tools isn't always the most pleasant experience. Now as creators and consumers of our own technological environment, we're pushing back against the three temptations of technology.

Temptation #1. Anything you *can* do with technology you *should* do with technology. This is the temptation my two friends at the bar were talking about. Yes, it is possible to create a social entrepreneur's browser and embed in it every hip application on the Web. But the question isn't "Can we do it?" The question is "Will it make our lives easier or more complicated? Solve a problem or cause a problem?" Technology for the sake of technology usually fails. What always fails is technology that takes a relatively simple human activity, such as cooking in a kitchen oven, and makes it more complicated than it needs to be—for example, building an oven that talks to you as you cook in it. Yes, there is such an oven. No, you don't really want one.

Temptation #2. If some is good, then more is better. If you want to see this principle in action, study the variety wars in Japan in the 1980s. What happened was, in a word, simple. Having learned how to create a production system that allowed almost unlimited variety, Japanese manufacturers went crazy. Sony offered 250 varieties of Walkman-like products; Sanyo produced refrigerators in twenty-four different colors with a two-week delivery time; Matsushita built 220 different types of TVs and 62 versions of VCRs. Faced with endless choice and rapid-fire new product releases, customers stopped buying: they were exhausted. Finally so were the producers, and the whole system collapsed under its own competitive insanity.

Temptation #3. Customers want choice, so we have to give it to them. Well, yes—and no. What customers really want is meaningful choice, or, at a minimum, less meaningless choice. We want choices that make our lives easier, simpler, and calmer. Remember Rule #2: we want things that work, that can be made to work better, that are new and innovative. We want to buy a car with less hassle and more transparency. We want software that installs itself. We want a cell phone that works—every time, everywhere. We want fewer buttons, not more. We want easy service arrangements—for an oil change, a cable box, a doctor's visit.

Yes, choice is good. But what we really want is to choose what kinds of things we get to choose.

So What?

Mastering the art of simplicity gives you a valuable edge. It means you've rejected the siren song of complexity, which often masquerades as sophistication or erudition. Instead you've practiced the hard work of finding the essence of your idea. Here are a few things to keep in mind.

1. **Simple is hard.** The reason simplicity looks simple is that someone has done the hard work of removing all

the complexity. It's easy to leave things messy and com-plicated. Simplicity takes hours of concentrated effort. I learned this by watching my wife when she worked as an architect and planner at Skidmore, Owings and Merrill. She spent endless hours going over the design specs she had to work with, more hours generating options, more hours combining and refining those options—and even then she didn't settle for one solu-tion. She wanted to see which options the client liked best before she generated her final design. Nothing is simple the first time through, or even the second. End-less repetition and self-editing reveal the simplicity hidden in the complexity.

2. One too many is still too many. As an editor, nothing made me happier than sticking my nose into the maga-zine's design. I'd stand behind Patrick Mitchell at *Fast Company* and watch him design the cover. After he'd finished, we'd always have the same discussion.

"Couldn't you add one more thing?" I'd ask. "It's missing something."

"Like what?" Patrick would ask back.

"I don't know," I'd say. "Maybe another color? One more touch?"

Patrick would say, "You know that point where you're designing a page and you're about to add one more thing?"

"Yes," I'd say.

"Don't."

His message was always the same: when in doubt, leave it out. Less is more and more is too much.

3. **Try it yourself.** How much is enough? How complicated is too complicated? Ultimately you have to be your own best critic. What happens when you try out your own new piece of software? How does it feel to check out at the new self-service grocery line? What happens when you dial the 800 help line? That feeling in your chest is called anxiety. That buzzing in your head is called confusion. If you feel them, you can be sure your customer does too. The goal of simplicity is to eliminate all those unpleasant emotions from the customer experience.

4. **Always remember the do-nothing alternative.** Part of the environmental impact statement process that flourished in the 1970s was a requirement that every project consider the do-nothing alternative: what if you simply didn't do the project at all? When you're considering simplicity it's always a good idea to go back to the most basic option of all, the do-nothing alternative, and see how it would change the way you're thinking about the design or implementation of your project.

5. **Complexity is an opportunity.** The world is a deeply tangled place—and likely to become more tangled in the future. We're all confronted with business and social issues that have more and more moving parts. That's a given. The question is, how do you cut through

the tangle and bring a simpler solution to people whose daily lives are already overtaxed and overstressed? Wherever you see complexity you also see opportunity. Just remember the conversation my young friends had in the bar: "Will it make my life easier?" Because there's no point in taking a situation that's already complicated and piling your complications on top of that. No point, no benefit, and no future.

THE RED AUERBACH MANAGEMENT PRINCIPLE: LOYALTY IS A TWO-WAY STREET.

There was more to St. Louis than baseball back in the late 1950s and early 1960s. That was the heyday of the rivalry between the St. Louis Hawks and the Boston Celtics. All my friends were big Hawks fans, but my brother and I learned to love the Celtics. We'd go down to the old Arena, buy cheap tickets in the nosebleed section, and watch the Hawks of Pettit, Hagan, Martin, Lovelette, and McMahon do battle with the Celtics of Russell, the Jones boys, Heinsohn, Ramsay, and Cousy.

As the game wound down, when Boston was winning, our eyes would turn from the players on the court to the man on the Celtics' bench. With his program wound into a cylinder and a rumpled suit that made him look more like Willy Loman than the world's greatest basketball mind, Arnold "Red" Auerbach, the celebrated coach of the Celtics, would watch until the game was safely won. Then and only then he'd break out his trademark: a victory cigar. When he lit up it meant the game was over. It was a sign of contentment and,

I suspect, a way he had of sticking it to the opposition, especially on the road. I just thought it was cool.

Which explains my plan, thirty years later when I was running *HBR*, to interview Red Auerbach on his management philosophy. I'd already interviewed former heads of state. Why not sit down with a man who'd won sixteen NBA championships and held the jobs of coach, general manager, and president of one of the most storied franchises in all of sports? Why not satisfy a childhood dream at the same time?

On the day of our appointment I found my way to his office. With no fanfare or formality his assistant ushered me in. He was sitting behind his desk. The office was messy, small, and unpretentious. This was 1987, before sports took on the trappings of big-money business. No plush practice facilities, private jets, or flashy executive suites. This was Red Auerbach's brand of basketball, not Mark Cuban's.

He waited for me to set up my tape recorder and then he offered me a cigar. A Red Auerbach cigar! The kind he used to celebrate victories! And I—I!—said no thanks. Not because I didn't want one or because I didn't smoke cigars. I didn't want him to know what a complete groupie I was. I was too embarrassed to take it—which explains how I missed out having a Red Auerbach cigar in my sports memorabilia collection.

But if I missed out on the cigar, the interview itself is etched in my memory. More than anything I remember the clear and slow way he talked. He pronounced his words with a kind of sticky, syrupy quality that I associated with a mouth that has smoked a lot of cigars. He practically chewed each word, producing it in the way a veteran smoker produces smoke rings. The way he spoke gave his words the feeling that each one was the subject of careful consideration. There was nothing glib about Red Auerbach. He was the opposite of today's slick motivator with pseudo-psychological patter. He wasn't big or aggressive. But sitting across from me, he seemed burly, a bear-like man whose words rolled across the desk the way an old-time boxer would roll across the ring. Not menacing, but mentally tough, direct, and forceful.

It turned into a great interview. According to *HBR* lore, when it appeared in the March-April 1987 issue, someone at McKinsey found it so compelling they ordered reprints for the entire firm. What did Red say to warrant that reaction?

You don't reward your players based on their statistics—you reward them based on their contributions to the team. "I don't believe in statistics," Red said. "You can't measure a ball-player's heart, his ability to perform in the clutch, his willingness to sacrifice his offense or to play strong defense."

You create a special bond with your players based on honesty. "The players won't con me because I won't con them," he told me. "They don't give me what I call false hustle, when a guy just goes through the motions but he's not really putting out much effort."

You never motivate your players through fear but only through pride. "We like our players to play for fun and to be happy rather than afraid," he said. "It's like that in any business. If you have employees who work through fear, you're not going to get any ingenuity out of them."

Uncertainty creates a huge problem for professional athletes—and a huge opportunity for coaches. "You see, in sports you have so many things that aren't expected," Red said. "There's so much uncertainty. So when players find themselves in a situation where management has a great deal of integrity and they can depend on my word or anybody else's word in the organization, they feel secure. And if the players feel secure, they don't want to leave here. And if they don't want to leave here, they're going to do everything they can on the court to stay here."

But the single most memorable management tip he gave me was this: *loyalty is a two-way street.* When I asked him to explain the Celtics' mystique, he said: "One important thing is trust within our organization. I really believe that loyalty is a two-way street. Unfortunately, in most businesses managers expect loyalty from employees but are very reluctant to give loyalty. We've built up an organization where we care about our people. That doesn't mean that you can't make trades. You must have a certain amount of flexibility so if you feel you can improve your club, you go ahead and make a trade. But over the years we've made very few trades. Anybody who's been with us for more than five or six years will usually finish his career here. And when a player is on the tail end of his career, we don't just say, 'We paid you, you played. See you later.' "

That's why a facsimile of Red's signature is on the Celtics' parquet floor today—because Red left his signature on the whole franchise.

So What?

It's hard to improve on the managerial wisdom of an iconic coach who won 938 games in his NBA career.

So let me simply underscore his words on loyalty: he's right. Most business managers act as though they were entitled to loyalty from their employees but somehow don't believe they're equally responsible for showing loyalty to their employees.

It seems clear in retrospect that Dan Pink's "free agent nation" movement of the 1990s was an entirely logical response to Michael Hammer's reengineering craze of the 1980s. People, it turns out, aren't actually stupid. When employees saw the princely sums their employers were paying consultants to figure out how to reengineer them out of their jobs, they reached the only logical conclusion: if the company isn't loyal to me, why should I be loyal to it? By declaring themselves free agents, talented men and women in the knowledge economy could negotiate the way free agents in the new world of sports did: they'd play for the highest bidder until an even higher bidder came along. Businesses were taking the low road in the way they treated their workers and creating the same conditions Auerbach was criticizing in the NBA.

What's the explanation?

Are companies so profoundly worried that their workers will somehow take unfair advantage of them that they decide to strike first so there's no doubt who's the boss?

Are managers afraid their peers or their bosses will think they're weak if they don't adopt a punitive approach to their employees?

Is it a function of short-term economics? A product of managers being held to their numbers and so taking exactly the opposite of Auerbach's approach, which was never to trust the statistics, never to believe the numbers?

Whatever the reason, the failure of American companies to make loyalty a two-way street has opened up for some the same opportunity seized on by Auerbach and the Celtics. What Auerbach did was to position the Celtics as the anti-reengineering sports franchise, the team players could count on to treat them with respect, fairness, and dignity. To be a valued and valuable member of this team you didn't have to score a lot of points. You had to be a team player and be willing to contribute. It was Auerbach, after all, who invented the concept of role players and "the sixth man"—the player good enough to start but who was willing to come off the bench to contribute a jolt of energy the other team couldn't counter.

One last story Auerbach told me was his deal with Bill Walton. Walton contacted Auerbach about coming to play for the Celtics. But once he was with the team, Walton became troubled because he wasn't scoring more points. Auerbach put him at ease by telling him his contribution to the team would be measured not in how many points he scored but in all the ways he contributed to the team winning.

Who wouldn't want to play for a coach like that? Who wouldn't want to be part of a team like that?

More to the point, who wouldn't want to learn to be a manager like that?

MESSAGE TO ENTREPRENEURS: MANAGING YOUR EMOTIONAL FLOW IS MORE CRITICAL THAN MANAGING YOUR CASH FLOW.

If you look up the term "cash flow" in the annals of entrepreneurial conventional wisdom, what you find is, well, conventional wisdom.

"Cash is king!"

"Cash flow is the lifeblood of any business."

"Cash is the essential fuel that powers an entrepreneurial business."

Got it? "King." "Lifeblood." "Essential fuel." Whether you prefer royalty, medicine, or energy as your business metaphor of choice, the point is the same: when it comes to entrepreneurship nothing is more vital than cash.

My own entry in the annals is different: *the biggest threat to any start-up isn't running out of money—it's going out of your mind.* Here's how I found out.

It took Bill Taylor and me more than three years to go from business plan to launch of *Fast Company*. That's three-plus years of two guys sitting in a room talking to each other about how to start a magazine. Two type A personalities, highly competitive, prone to mood swings, and enormously critical of self and others. Three-plus years of seeking and getting advice from anyone who was willing to offer it, of getting meetings with anyone who could offer help. Three-plus years of imagining stories for a magazine that didn't yet exist, of designing direct mail tests without a product to send to potential subscribers.

It was three-plus years of emotional ups and downs.

Bill and I would have a good meeting with someone offering encouragement and all of a sudden we could visualize the finish line looming ahead. Then we'd have a bad meeting and our spirits would plunge into the slough of despond.

I remember getting a phone call out of the blue from the head of the *Economist* in London. A mutual friend, a professor at HBS, had put in a good word for our magazine project, and this British gentleman with a hyphenated last name was calling to find out more. I was so excited, I blurted out how eager Bill and I were to make a deal with him—and I could hear the air go out of the phone call. After I hung up I could smell the cordite from shooting myself in the foot.

It was excruciatingly painful—a constant battle to achieve some semblance of emotional equilibrium.

We were looking for money, but our struggle wasn't about money (notwithstanding Bruce Springsteen's gritty reminder that "sooner or later it all comes down to money"). It was about sanity. Every day hung in the balance. Every decision mattered. Every step was fateful, either in the right direction toward our ultimate goal or in the wrong direction toward total oblivion. That emotional pressure meant that every day was subject to the same kind of intense scrutiny that soothsayers used to give to the entrails of sacrificial animals.

It's also what made Bill and me such perfect partners. We complemented each other both in our thinking and in our emotional metabolism: we were a sine curve and a cosine curve teamed up as partners. Our ups and downs were perfectly offsetting. On average we were calm, stable, and able to face each day without surrendering to the pressures of failure.

What we learned was that our first job was staying sane; our second job was finding the money. After all, what doth it profit a man if he gaineth the world but loseth his mind?

So What?

It was during this sojourn in the desert that I grew fond of a Woody Allen saying: "More than any time in history mankind faces a crossroads. One path leads to despair and hopelessness, the other to total extinction. Let us pray that we have the wisdom to choose correctly." That's my idea of entrepreneurial humor.

But the crucible of entrepreneurship does teach lessons hard and soft. Here are a few things I learned.

Entrepreneurship is a state of mind. It's more about a way of being and thinking about yourself than a way of creating economic opportunity. That's why would-be entrepreneurs need to give as much preparation to the psychological demands of their chosen way of life as they do to the financial demands. If you can't manage the stress of uncertainty, ambiguity, and doubt, your skill at managing cash flow won't matter.

Remember that there is nothing more difficult than

trying to will something new into existence. Think about it. Your idea currently doesn't exist—and the world isn't missing it. Now you are going to use all your powers of persuasion and all your skills to convince the world it desperately needs what it isn't missing. It's an amazing act to conjure something out of nothing. It's an act of courage. You have to believe in your idea, but first you have to believe in yourself. All the hours that Bill and I spent together practicing our lines for meetings with others prepared us to launch the magazine—because we were practicing our belief in ourselves.

So if entrepreneurship isn't some let's-go-find-a-garage-and-start-the-next-big-thing romp and instead is a soul-searching trial by fire, what are a few things to keep in mind as you book your passage to your own personal destiny?

1. **"Team, team, team."** That's what Kleiner Perkins' John Doerr told me when I asked him how he decided on investments in start-ups. It's not the spreadsheet—nobody believes those numbers. It's who's on the team. I know I couldn't have sustained my own sanity without Bill Taylor. He made things happen; he supplied down-to-earth focus to bring *Fast Company* into existence. On top of pure genius he provided raw energy. So the first thing I'd advise any aspiring entrepreneur is to find your Bill Taylor—the perfect partner. It's a lonely journey as it is; find the right partner and both of you will have someone to depend on.

2. **Nothing's so serious that you can't laugh at it—especially yourself.** Bill and I still laugh about the time I

tried to call legendary Silicon Valley investor Art Rock and, using San Francisco information, got the number for Art Rock. When I called, they told me Art Rock was in jail. Shaken by the news, I told Bill; he wisely told me it couldn't be true and made me call back. It turned out I'd gotten the number for an art gallery—Art Rock—whose owner had been jailed for some art-related scam. Art Rock was, in fact, in jail, just not *the* Art Rock. By the time we actually launched *Fast Company* we had a catalog of hilarious moments, proof that when it comes to entrepreneurship, he who laughs, lasts.

3. Listen to lots of loud music—it will keep you pumped up. If you think it's hard to work with music playing, try surviving without it. We made it so much a part of our start-up culture that once *Fast Company* launched, Patrick Mitchell, our art director, produced an annual bootleg album: "Music to Magazine By." Very cool.

4. Entrepreneurs, like armies, travel on their bellies. When you're struggling against the odds to make something happen, making one part of each day completely reliable can mean a lot. It has a name: "lunch." In a world where everything else is complicated, make lunch simple. Wherever we moved our offices in the prelaunch phase of *Fast Company*—and we had a handful of makeshift offices before we managed a real one—we also established a regular place to eat lunch. We became regulars. Our orders became regular. The routine became regular. It was our still place in a turning universe, something we could count on to bring order to the day.

That's it, my prescription for entrepreneurial mental health: a great partner, lots of laughs, loud music, and comfort food.

Simple, right? So go start something! And stay sane.

ALL MONEY IS NOT CREATED EQUAL.

Y ou've written and rewritten your business plan. You've developed an airtight business case for your idea. You've taken out as much risk as you can: strategic risk, competitive risk, technological risk, human risk.

Check, check, check, check.

Which brings us to checks.

It's time to raise your first round of money.

Suddenly the prospect of looking for money feels daunting. Where to start? Whom to ask first? Friends and family? Venture capitalists—the people your friends insist on calling "vulture capitalists"?

Here's how we raised our first round to beta-test *Fast Company.*

Our initial determination was to do it right. For us, doing it right began with a simple idea: all money is not created equal.

It's true it all spends the same. But who you get it from makes all the difference. Some money is smart and some dumb; some comes untethered and some has strings attached; some is patient and some will frazzle you. Some money comes from people you're proud to associate with, and some money is associated with people you'd rather not admit you know. There's strategic money that opens up multiple opportunities, and there's money that is only money. You need to know the different kinds of money.

With that in mind, we had our legal papers drawn up. (The biggest mistake you can make with your start-up is to scrimp on getting a great lawyer—a natural reaction, because you haven't raised any money yet. But when your idea works, the money you spent on a great lawyer will make you a lot more money. Whenever an entrepreneur asks me for advice, I always offer the same two words: call Irwin. That's Irwin Heller in Boston.)

Then we created the specs for our first-round investors. We wanted qualified investors, people who could afford to lose their investment if the magazine didn't work. And we told them up front that magazines ranked along with restaurants and Broadway shows when it came to risk.

We wanted people who had more than financial capital; we wanted people with reputational capital—people whose credibility would give us credibility.

We wanted our investors to embody the concept at the heart of the magazine. The magazine was all about innovation and fresh thinking, and we wanted people who stood for those qualities. That meant cutting-edge entrepreneurs and venture capitalists, and thought leaders in business schools and management consulting firms.

We wanted people who had their own circles of influential friends. We wanted access to their Rolodexes. Who better than friends of our investors to subscribe to the magazine they'd financed?

Fast Company was going to be global, so we wanted our group of investors to include people outside the United States.

We wanted people with ideas to contribute on top of everything else. We didn't want them to dictate editorial policy. But if they were thought leaders, why not get their thoughts in our pages?

And finally we wanted people who got it. They had to enjoy the idea that they were founding investors in a fun but risky enterprise. No whiners need apply.

That was our version of a first-round Rubik's Cube. We had our half-dozen criteria; our assignment was to click them all in place to come up with the right group of people to provide the right amount of money.

Our goal was $450,000. It took us nine months to hit it and we not only got the right amount of money but also got the right team of investors. Our first-round investors gave us everything we needed to get started—and down the road their credibility helped us make the deal to get the magazine launched. So here's a toast to *Fast Company*'s Rubik's Cube of investors: John Abele, B. Charles Ames, Thomas P. Axworthy, John Doerr, Mark B. Fuller, Martin Goldfarb, Junichi Hattori, Harry Hopmeyer, Regis McKenna, Peter Nicholas, Andrall Pearson, Tom Peters, Michael Porter, Neil Raymond, George Stalk, and Hirotaka Takeuchi.

In the end, starting a business is more about getting the right people to invest than it is about getting their money.

So What?

The search for money will drive you crazy if you let it. Don't let it.

Start by remembering that you're looking for more than money. You're looking to build the next leg of your overall launch strategy. To do that you need your own design specs to figure out what kinds of money you want. From the design specs you can figure out who best meets them. So start by asking the kinds of questions that will produce the specs that fit your entrepreneurial idea.

How much money do you need and what's a reasonable amount to ask each investor to put in? (Here's a hypothetical to test your strategy: if one investor offered to put up the whole amount you need, would that help or hurt your chances of success?)

Assume you'll raise the money. What kinds of people will help you most when you launch? Are there professions or industries that should be represented in your investment group?

What other criteria will help make the case for your project? Age, gender, race, nationality, religion, other affiliation? Go back to the metaphor of running for office: whose endorsement would help your project succeed? When you go to the next leg of your launch, what claims do you want to be able to make about your backers?

When you've answered those questions you'll have your specs and your specs will produce names of investors.

Now comes the hard part: time to look the devil in the eye. Here are some rules for asking for money.

If it's your project, you make the ask. Delegating it to someone else is a coward's way out. Remember, your investors aren't investing in your idea—they're investing in you. So you have to be the one to ask for the money.

To make the ask, go see them, preferably at their office. This is work; it's serious. Bring them a copy of the business plan if you haven't sent it ahead. If you trust them enough to ask them for money, trust them with your business plan. (Although there's nothing wrong with also bringing along a nondisclosure agreement as protection. It also shows you're serious.)

Practice your pitch. Make it short, clear, and direct. Above all, make the ask. Explicitly. When it comes to money, there's nothing worse than leading up to the big question and then not having the guts to pop it: "I'm looking for investors to start my company and I'd love to have you in the group. I'm looking for [your amount goes here]. Can I count on you to invest?" Just say it! If you don't ask, don't expect the investor to make the pitch for you.

If the answer is no, learn to take no for an answer. (And as a question.) Of course, you don't have to make it easy. You don't have to say, "If you can't do it, I completely understand." But if they can't, they can't. You still have to thank them.

If they can, be prepared. Have the papers to sign; if you can go home with their check, take the check. (Remember, nothing happens until money changes hands—see Rule #9.)

And if they do say yes, then, as Rick said in *Casablanca*, you're at the beginning of a beautiful friendship. Check in hand, you're now responsible for managing that relationship. You owe your investors regular updates and progress reports. Not as an obligation, but as a business relationship. Your first-round investors are the booster rockets to your ultimate launch. Because they're more than just money to you, you have to be more than just an investment to them.

It's not only the right way to do business. It's the way to succeed at business.

IF YOU WANT TO THINK BIG, START SMALL.

I'm sitting in Stockholm in the open room that serves as the catchall meeting space for the Swedish branch of the KaosPilots—"the best school *for* the world." More chairs are set up than usual. There's an inner circle of chairs for the students and a second, outer circle for friends, family, and supporters. Today is a special day: Nobel Peace Prize winner Muhammad Yunus is visiting the KaosPilots. These young students are paying their own tuition rather than attend one of Sweden's many state-funded colleges because they want to learn the skills of a social innovator. Who better to learn from than Muhammad Yunus?

Yunus isn't one for speeches. He sits quietly at the front of the room under the banner with the playful KaosPilots logo and invites questions from the students. He's so down-to-earth, honest, matter-of-fact, and authentic that it takes only a few awkward opening questions from the slightly awed students before they forget that the man dressed in his signature Bangladeshi vest is the founder of the Grameen Bank and a genuine Nobel laureate.

Yunus goes around the circle inviting each student to ask

a question. Finally, one student asks the question that many have been thinking.

"There's so many things that concern me, so many problems that need working on," she says. "I don't know where to start. Global warming, poverty, AIDS. Where do you think I should start?"

It's the question of a generation that genuinely wants to change the world. But in a world that needs so much changing, the biggest problem is getting started.

Yunus' answer is simple, direct, and practical.

"Start with whatever is right in front of you," he advises. "Start with whatever is within your reach. That's how I got started. With one woman who needed a little bit of money to get out from underneath a loan shark."

He takes a few minutes to recount the grassroots origins of what later became the Grameen Bank. A famine struck Bangladesh shortly after the country gained independence. One morning, in the village of Jobra, Yunus came across Sufiya Begum, an impoverished woman, sitting in her muddy yard crafting small stools out of bamboo. Yunus asked her why, despite her hard work, she was still living in poverty. The answer: she could borrow the money to buy the bamboo for her furniture only from a loan shark who also bought all she produced at a price he set. She was in virtual economic slavery. After a week of research Yunus learned there were forty-two other people in the village in the same circumstances. Together they owed the loan shark less than $27—a small sum, perhaps, but more than they could afford. Yunus went to the local bank to see if it would provide loans to rescue the families from the loan shark. The bank said it couldn't loan money to those people—they were poor! Finally, with $27 from his own pocket, Yunus freed the forty-two families from the loan shark. It was the first small step toward the birth of the Grameen Bank.

It's a familiar story, but hearing it from Yunus' own mouth makes one thing profoundly clear: Muhammad Yunus didn't set out from home one morning with the goal of ending poverty in Bangladesh or raising tens of millions of people around the world out of poverty. He wasn't thinking about starting a bank or a social movement. He certainly wasn't game-planning how to win the Nobel Peace Prize. He saw a woman in a village who needed help and, as he told the students in Stockholm, "I could not not help her."

It started out, in other words, as a solution in a petri dish, like so many other world-changing social projects. What it offers is an instructive model for crafting solutions that work, one that applies equally well to for-profit and not-for-profit entrepreneurs.

Start small. Do what you can with something you care about so deeply that you simply can't not do it. Stay focused, close to the ground, rooted in everyday reality. Trust your instincts and your eyes: do what needs doing any way you can, whether the experts agree or not. Put practice ahead of theory and results ahead of conventional wisdom.

Start small. If it works, keep doing it. If it doesn't work, change what you're doing until you find something that does work. Start small, start with whatever is close at hand, start with something you care deeply about. But as Muhammad Yunus told the KaosPilots, start.

So What?

"Get big or get out." That's conventional wisdom when it comes to venture-capital-backed Web start-ups.

There's another model emerging today, one made smarter, faster, and in some ways inevitable by the Web. Think of it as the Muhammad Yunus approach to change.

It starts with small experiments undertaken by people who aren't experts—which may be their key advantage. They don't accept what the experts have already decided: for instance, that you can't loan money to poor people. They don't know that it takes an ironclad business plan before you can launch your project. They don't know that bigger is better. They do know that they're determined to make a difference.

It's a model that Yunus personifies, one that he spreads wherever he goes and whenever he speaks. On one occasion he spoke at Stanford University and in the audience was Jessica Jackley. She heard Yunus talk about using microfinance to change the lives of people who were poor but had untapped entrepreneurial skills. That speech was the start.

In 2004, when she and her husband, Matt, had been married only a few months, Jessica flew to East Africa for the Village Enterprise Fund, interviewing entrepreneurs who had used grants of $100 to $150 to start their own businesses. Matt joined her for two weeks and filmed some of the interviews. What they saw convinced them that even the smallest loans could make a huge difference in the lives of poor people living in Africa.

When they got back to San Francisco they went to work,

figuring out how to build a microfinance bridge between people who wanted to help and people in rural Africa who needed help. Finally, after a year of sometimes frustrating discussions with experts, they decided that the best way to begin was simply to begin. In March 2005 Jessica and Matt launched their beta site. They raised $3,500 from about thirty-five people to make loans to seven Ugandan entrepreneurs, a Yunus-like beginning. Six months later, every loan had been repaid.

In October 2005 Jessica and Matt announced the world's first peer-to-peer microlending Web site: Kiva.org. In year one Kiva.org got $430,000 from 5,400 people and made loans to 750 people in twelve countries. Two years later Kiva.org had grown to a total of $39,536,810 spread over 55,935 loans, with funds coming from 329,406 lenders. Seventy-seven percent of the loans went to women entrepreneurs, and the repayment rate was 98.45 percent.

"With Kiva we had huge dreams but we were practical about getting started," Jessica says of starting Kiva.org. "We knew we had to begin with something specific and doable. In fact, I think that's the only way to start, period—small, specific, and focused. We're still a relatively small team, so we can be nimble, responsive, and innovative. Sometimes to address the big injustices in the world lots of tiny, context-specific, tailored solutions are appropriate."

I could have told you the story of Cameron Sinclair and Architecture for Humanity, or Sasha Chanoff and Mapendo International, or any one of the 150 nonprofits that are started every day in the United States as young people turn their attention from making as much money as possible to making as much change as possible.

Get big or get out?

How about start small and stick with it?

"SERIOUS FUN" ISN'T AN OXYMORON; IT'S HOW YOU WIN.

L et's take a look back at how work used to be.

The year is 1934 and we're in the offices of Brown Brothers Harriman, America's oldest privately held bank. The following memo goes out to the young men in the office:

"For the good of all concerned and for the general appearance of the Department, the following should be carefully noted:

1. Male members of the department are requested not to fool with the female clerks in the office but to conduct themselves at all times as gentlemen should.

2. Clerks may smoke before 9 A.M. and after 3:30 P.M.

3. Members of the department are requested not to go into other departments in the office unless on business. (With only time on your hands, please stay at your desk.)

4. Your desks and the entire department should be kept neat at all times."

Off to Detroit and 1940. John Gallo, an assembly line worker at the Ford Motor Company, is fired after being "caught in the act of smiling." Served him right: he'd already been warned once for "laughing with the other fellows." At Ford's assembly line, workers aren't allowed to hum, whistle, or talk with other workers, even during lunch breaks. Henry Ford's philosophy says, "When we are at work we ought to be at work. When we are at play we ought to be at play. There is no use trying to mix the two."

Now it's 1956 and William H. Whyte Jr. has been interviewing CEOs for his book *The Organization Man*. To get the kind of junior executives big companies want and avoid the misfits, corporate America relies on standardized tests. "If you want to get a high score," Whyte writes, "you will do well to observe these two rules:

1. When asked for word associations or comments about the world, give the most conventional, run-of-the-mill, pedestrian answer possible.

2. When in doubt about the most beneficial answer to any question, repeat to yourself:

I love my father and my mother, but my father a little bit more.

I like things pretty much the way they are.

I never worry much about anything.

I don't care for books or music much.

I love my wife and children.

I don't let them get in the way of company work.

"If you were this kind of person you wouldn't get very far," Whyte concludes, "but, unfortunately, you won't get very far unless you can seem to be this kind."

Time now to return to the present, where winning in business requires playful work and serious fun. Start this tour with Dan Pink's *A Whole New Mind*, a book that describes how we all need to think differently about work in a right-brained economy. Dan cites Southwest Airlines' mission statement as a direct contradiction to Henry Ford: "People rarely succeed at anything unless they are having fun doing it," says the airline. In addition to Southwest, Dan reports, more than fifty European companies have taught their people how to engage in "serious play," a technique designed to unlock creativity.

Serious play is what Andy Stefanovich's firm, Play, is all about. According to Andy, strategic play is "a process and a mind-set. It's all about looking for ideas rather than solutions, and focusing on possibilities versus realities. It's about unlearning what you've learned in the business world."

If you're looking for the antithesis of the 1950s organization man, test-for-conformity hiring system, it's Ivy Ross. The top marketer at the Gap and a member of the board of the National Institute of Play (yes, there is such a thing), Ivy has her own hiring test: when she interviews job seekers she uses *mien shiang*, an ancient Chinese face-reading technique. Once people make her team, it's Ivy's job to unlock their creativity—"and that means having conditions that encourage trust and freedom," she says.

Like what?

A Tibetan monk comes in and teaches her teams how to work as a living system. A sound theorist analyzes the vibrational frequency of her team and produces a CD that matches their collective pitch. When she's faced with a marketing problem, Ivy trusts her own training as an artist—her work is in twelve museums—to look deeply into the heart of the matter. At Mattel, for example, where she previously worked, the company needed to come up with an idea for a funny toy. But you can't produce a breakthrough funny toy unless you're willing to dig deeper into fun. Ivy started with the question "What is laughter?" To get at the answer—and ultimately create a breakthrough toy—Ivy brought in a professor of laughter from UCLA. The result? A big hit for Mattel and a confirmation for Ivy of how creativity works: "Relaxation, trust, and freedom—that's what it's all about."

So much for Brown Brothers Harriman, Ford, or 1950s corporate America. Business today is serious fun.

So What?

Is serious play a part of your workplace? Or are you mired back in the 1930s, 1940s, or 1950s? Here are a few things to work on or play with, depending on your point of view.

1. **Start with an internal audit.** How would you describe your company's culture? Are people excited to come to work? Or are they encouraged to leave their personali-

ties at the door? Which of these apply to your organization:

> a) Work is work, fun is fun, and never the twain shall meet.
>
> b) We don't really trust our people; if they think it's okay to have fun at work, they'll take advantage of us.
>
> c) Control—we must maintain control!
>
> d) If God had meant for us to have fun at work, He wouldn't have put starch in our shorts.
>
> e) [Your excuse goes here.]

2. What in your workplace encourages serious play? In Ivy's workspace the desks are on wheels so people can move around and form spontaneous teams. What kind of music, furniture, or hands-on material would give your teams a chance to work and play together?

3. Do you let your people go? No, I don't mean fire them—I mean the kind of "radical sabbaticals" that Andy Stefanovich offers at Play. People can volunteer for Habitat for Humanity, learn to play guitar, take a trip or a dance class, and come back inspired from their play to work more creatively.

4. Do you know how to celebrate? Most office parties feel awkward and insincere. But there's a lot to be said about a culture that knows how to celebrate its wins and recognize its people—and means it. Make celebration a part of how you do business and you'll do more business.

5. Where do you come together as a team? At *Fast Company* we had the 'Rang—a boomerang-shaped, bar-height table adjacent to the kitchen, where people gathered for lunch, coffee, or just to hang out. At *HBR*, we had . . . nowhere. Which magazine had a livelier culture and a more creative flow of ideas? If you want people to create together, give them a place to come together.

Having fun at work is serious stuff. And so is the old model of crushing the spirit of the people who work for you. Here's what management guru Bob Dylan has to say about soul-crushing corporate culture:

> "One of the boss's hangers-on
> Comes to call at times you least expect
> Try to bully ya—strongarm you—inspire you with fear
> It has the opposite effect."

You don't want to end up in a Bob Dylan song, do you? Time to get to work playfully.

TECHNOLOGY IS ABOUT CHANGING HOW WE WORK.

We have so much technology, we love it so much, and we depend on it for so many things. Maybe it's time to ask, what's the point of technology?

I got my first hint at an answer in 1989 when I went to Japan for three months as a Japan Society fellow. I got there just as the technological genie was leaving the bottle. It was still early in the game—fax machines were still a big deal back then—but I knew enough from what I saw to bring back my version of "I've seen the future and it works": the future was going to be personal, portable, and digital.

I went to interview Ricoh's CEO and he gave me a demonstration, moving a photo from a camera to a copy machine, from the copy machine to a computer, from the computer to the fax. All information—photos, sound, documents, you name it—would be digital. And once it was digital it could move seamlessly from platform to platform. It stood to reason that if boundaries between platforms were disappearing, then boundaries within an organization, or between organizations, between industries, or between nations would also disappear. Companies would get flatter as digital information collapsed levels; functions would converge as digital information connected them.

Moving the information around effortlessly meant it would belong to the user. No more central repository where it all had to be stored. We'd each have our own computer files and computer accounts. Information would be personal; work would be personal. We'd be released from the old constraints of where, when, and how we'd work.

Work would be portable. I imagined hordes of newly liberated Japanese salary men on their golf carts zipping around immaculately mowed fairways, answering their personal, portable mobile phones, pretending they were still glued to their desks. If work were personal, portable, and digital the old organization chart had to change. Power belonged to the person who had the best information and the most trust from coworkers—not the person with the biggest job title.

Personal, portable, and digital meant that ideas could move without interruption or interference. It meant that the idea of a knowledge economy could move from concept to reality.

So What?

A few thoughts on what technology means:

1. It's never about the technology—it's always about what the technology makes possible.

2. If you're not a techie, that's okay. You don't have to understand all the details of how it works.

3. However, you do have to embrace all the changes information technology will bring. You have to buy it,

try it, and live it. You don't have to get it, but you can't afford to get left behind.

4. If you are a techie, that's okay too. The fact that you're a digital native is an advantage—but don't get too comfortable.

5. Because your workplace advantage will be very short-lived, instead of coasting on your insider status, learn to translate techie-talk into business-talk. That way you'll always have a job.

6. Technology change is generational change. My techno-mentor Thornton May says there are four generations currently in the workforce, each with its own relationship to technology: a sixty-year-old *uses* a PC; a forty-year-old *needs* a PC, always; a twenty-year-old *needs* connectivity, always; and to those under twenty an Xbox *is* technology. The point is, when it comes to technological change at work, it's always going to be a moving target.

7. When you say "technology" most people think of something they can touch, hold, or install: a computer, a chip, a router, or a piece of software. The real stuff of technology is invisible: it's the connections it creates, the speed and flexibility it enables, the changes in behavior it produces, and the possibilities for innovation it inspires. If you want to see the real power of technology look at what you can't see.

8. Another reason not to look too hard at the physical shapes technology takes is that most things, from the telephone to the laser to the Internet, don't get used for the purpose for which they were invented. The inventor creates the technology, and then we find uses for it. It's better to think of the uses of technology than the pieces of technology: computing is more important than the computer.

9. Contrary to popular belief, technology is neither the problem nor the solution. Technology is never a measure of itself and always a measure of us. Every technologist I've ever met, including a handful of Nobel Prize winners, urgently wants nonscientists to weigh in on the proper uses of their discoveries. They are desperate for conversations between scientists and ethicists, between technologists and politicians. Business leaders owe us at least the same level of self-awareness about their technological innovations. Every discovery has unintended consequences. No matter what we choose, technology won't let us come out the same way we went in. But we might as well try to make informed choices about how it changes us and the way we use it to work.

IF YOU WANT TO BE A REAL LEADER, FIRST GET REAL ABOUT LEADERSHIP.

Next to shopping, America's favorite indoor sport must be leadership training and development. One business magazine reported that in 2003 134 companies sent 21,000 employees to leadership training programs at a combined cost of $210 million. Other estimates put the amount spent on leadership training worldwide in the billions of dollars. For those inclined to do-it-yourself leadership development Amazon offers 284,928 titles in its leadership library (not counting this one).

At *Fast Company* we had a healthy skepticism toward America's traditional view of leadership. I thought the way it was written about in business magazines and books tended to idealize the image of the leader as a larger-than-life heroic figure. I used to make fun of other business magazines for their cover photos that invariably consisted of "white men facing right"—a time-tested formula for sell-through on the newsstand. Instead we developed an appreciation not for leaders—men in high places—but for people who demonstrated real leadership qualities. People who did what leaders do. Our leadership logic went something like this:

• We don't worship the people at the top simply because they are at the top. (There goes my invitation to Davos.)

• Organizations have gotten too big, the world too complicated, decisions too intricate, and change too rapid for any one person at the top to have all the answers.

• The job of the leader isn't to have all the answers.

• The job of the leader is to ask the right questions.

• More and more work is teamwork.

• Teamwork requires people who can take on the real work of leading at all levels of the organization.

• The company with the most leaders at all levels wins.

What is required is grassroots leadership—not an oxymoron, but a new way of looking at the work of being a leader.

Leadership isn't attached to any single job title. It doesn't come with a diploma, a degree, or a program. Leadership is a way of thinking and acting. A way of being and doing.

So What?

What is the real work of leading? If you want to get real about leadership, you can boil it down to four things: how leaders are, what leaders do, how leaders act, and what leaders leave behind them. Let's look at them one at a time.

How Leaders Are. There is a kind of leader we'd all like to follow, a model for the kind of leader we'd all like to be. What describes such people is a way of being. It starts with being both confident and modest. Jim Collins comments on this extensively: the leaders who took their companies from good to great knew both how good they were and how to check their egos at the door. A second key attribute: authenticity. We're all drawn to people who know who they are, who are comfortable in their own skins. Their sense of themselves makes it easier for us to know and trust them. It cuts down on the wasted energy and head games that too often accompany people in power who are at war with themselves—and take it out on us. Finally, good leaders are good listeners, as the Kennedy School's Ron Heifetz points out. They bring out the best in the people around them; they let others contribute and feel involved in deciding the direction and future of the company. "Too many leaders die with their mouths open," Ron says. Leaders who need to talk all the time create companies where people simply stop listening.

What Leaders Do. At the top of every real leader's list of things to do is "attract and grow talent." The team that has the most leaders at all levels of the organization wins. That means leading is a lot like coaching: taking talented but sometimes raw people and nurturing their development. You start with a dose of reality: decisions have real consequences, results matter, and performance counts. But there are also times when the leader has to take the heat for a mistake an employee has made—that's part of what makes the leader a leader and helps the employee grow into one. Leaders help people face reality and protect them when they need some cover.

Leaders lead by example. *Knowing it ain't the same as doing it.* Leaders who do it instead of just talk about it model leadership every day. What they do day in and day out becomes a source of education and inspiration for the people who work for them.

Leaders challenge their people to do their best work. The best leaders have high standards. They hold themselves to those standards and expect those who work for them to perform to those standards. After a real leader has moved on, the people who worked for him or her always say, "I learned more and did more than I ever thought I could."

How Leaders Act. Real leaders give their people guidance, not answers. They create guidelines and then allow their employees to fit their own answers into the template. Real leaders create an agenda, offer criteria, and describe a strategy to take the company ahead. Then they challenge their people to fill in the tactics and techniques to get the work done. As part of this process, real leaders always stop to learn from mistakes. Just as the military uses after-action reviews to assess combat performance and learn from mistakes, confident leaders sit down with their people to assess the results of every decision, whether it's considered a success or a failure. Over time that's how the company gets better.

What Leaders Leave Behind. Michael Abrashoff, the charismatic captain of the USS *Benfold* whom we profiled in *Fast Company*, had a simple question he'd ask business leaders, based on his own experience in the Navy: "When you leave your job—and you will leave someday—how do you want your troops to remember you? With cheers because they were so glad to see you go, or with tears because of how much you meant to them?"

What is the legacy a real leader leaves?

Passion for the business, a love of the company, and the commitment to leave it healthier and stronger than he or she found it.

A team of great people: if you've hired and developed great people and taught them how to work together as a strong team, you can say you've done your job as a real leader.

Articulating sound values and instilling them in the way the company does business. What does the company stand for? What does it believe? It does a leader little honor to reward the shareholders with outsized earnings and the executives with outlandish bonuses only to see the whole thing implode when it turns out the books were cooked.

And finally, real leaders make more leaders. If the company with the most and best leaders wins, the real leader is the one who makes more leaders at all levels of the organization. Leaders practice leadership to cultivate more leaders. That's what real leaders leave behind: more people who are real leaders.

THE SURVIVAL OF THE FITTEST IS THE BUSINESS CASE FOR DIVERSITY.

There's not much to see at Olduvai Gorge. You can sit on a bench with a canopy overhead to protect you from the Tanzanian sun and hear a short talk about the different strata at which Mary and Louis Leakey discovered evidence of some of our earliest ancestors. You can walk through a small museum and stand in front of a plaster cast of Lucy's footprints. But when you look over the edge down into the gorge itself you have to use your imagination to remind yourself: this is where it started for us. This is our shared ancestral home. Thinking about it that way makes the hair stand up on the back of your neck.

I was in Tanzania on a hybrid safari—part adventure, part "inventure." The adventure part was led by Daudi Peterson, whose travel company and charitable foundation focus on helping the surviving indigenous tribes maintain their history and culture. During the day Daudi introduced us to the animals and wildlife of Tanzania and brought us into the lives of the Maasai, Hadzabe, and Dorobo tribes. At night around the campfire we had our "inventure" as Richard Leider led us through a series of exercises designed to encourage us to take stock of our work and our lives back in America.

"The survival laws of Africa are pretty simple," Daudi and Richard said. "Eat. Don't get eaten. Have sex to reproduce." They paused for a beat. "We won't be doing the last one."

The survival laws are never far from your mind, however, when you look down into Olduvai Gorge, travel across the Serengeti, and experience the everyday life of the tribespeople. We descended into the Ngorongoro Crater, an environment so strong you can feel the evolutionary forces at work. In this real-life Jurassic Park, alive with glorious wildlife, 80 percent of the animals die in their first year of life—food for the ones who survive.

Not far from there I got to experience the real world of our ancestral hunter-gatherers. I went digging with Hadzabe women and their digging sticks, chopping at the base of small bushes, unearthing tubers that we cooked over an open bonfire. That was the gathering part of a way of life that goes back more than sixty thousand years. The next day I got a chance to participate in the hunting part—walking for six hours behind a Hadzabe hunter who was armed with a bow and poisoned arrows. I came back with speargrass in both feet; he came back with a guinea fowl he'd shot through the neck and a family of redbills he'd scooped out of their nest. That night the tribe would eat fresh meat. A few days later I watched one of the last three Dorobo tribesmen stalk an impala—only three Dorobo left on the planet, and all of them men. Eat, don't get eaten, have sex to reproduce. The Dorobo had violated the third law of survival.

At night I'd lie awake under the blanket of stars in the

Southern Hemisphere, stars I never saw in the United States, and wonder what was going on back home—and back in corporate America. Lying in my sleeping bag, I tried to make the connection between the green hills of Africa and the white cubicles of America. What were we trying to achieve in those office buildings and factories? The people here knew exactly what they were trying to achieve. It wasn't sophisticated; it didn't promise a high standard of living. But it was elemental and unambiguous. They were trying to preserve a way of life. Every day was about one thing: survival.

What were we all about? How did survival fit in? Did it? Or was it submerged so far below the surface that we'd lost touch with that primal instinct?

For the first time I could see a company as a tribe, a group of people joined together to create a way of living that could continue into the future. Like the Hadzabe, companies are their people, living communities trying to make it another day, living according to the principles of biology and the laws of Charles Darwin.

Survival of the fittest. Survival, not of the strongest or richest, but of the most adaptable. Survival of the species with a gene pool diverse enough to keep it from becoming more and more specialized to conditions less and less likely to continue. A diverse gene pool could prevent a species—or a company—from driving headlong into a dead-end future.

You could think of a diverse gene pool as an insurance policy for change. And you could think of Charles Darwin as the most important management guru for business today.

The case for diversity used to rest on doing what was right. Our values argue for diversity. Our moral code tells us that equal opportunity is the American way of doing business. But at night in Tanzania I began to see another case for diversity: survival of the fittest. A diverse population gives any organization its best shot at survival. When change is rapid and unpredictable, diversity offers a chance at adaptation.

On the plains of Africa there are bigger, stronger, faster, fiercer animals than we poor, scrawny human beings. But we've made it—so far—by being smarter, more collaborative, more inventive, and more social than these other animals. We work together. We find common purpose across our differences. It is the survival of the fittest.

So What?

We're living through a period of unprecedented change. Companies will change because they have to—or face extinction. Diversity is the key to adaptation and the ticket to the future. Diversity is your way of tapping new ideas. It's a way of learning new ways of thinking and operating. It opens lines to new markets and new customers.

Take a look around you. Check your team, your department, your board. Who's missing? Knowing what you already know about how the world is changing, who needs to be in the room, at the table—but isn't? What skills, background, gender, geography, race, religion, culture, do you need so your gene pool is well mixed for the future?

Demographics tell us that very soon American minorities will, in fact, be the majority. When you want to learn more about Hispanic culture and tastes, for example, whom in your organization do you turn to? Evidence continues to pile up that women lead the way in consumer purchasing decisions. Where in your company are women in power? Brazil, Russia, India, and China are the economic bloc of the future. Who in your company knows these nations, can speak their languages, can translate their cultural and religious traditions for you? Face the facts of your own corporate gene pool: are you courting extinction through uniformity? Is your hiring policy based on the laws of the EEOC—or the laws of nature? Starting today, natural selection should describe your hiring strategy.

Diversity isn't a matter of ideology or morality. It's a pragmatic survival strategy, a sensible response to dramatic change. Companies that resist embracing diversity do so at their own peril—not only because it puts them on the wrong side of society, but also because it puts them on the wrong side of nature. Diversity as a matter of survival traces back to the deepest reservoirs of our human experience, all the way from Olduvai Gorge to the corporate boardroom.

DON'T CONFUSE CREDENTIALS WITH TALENT.

The bank was one of the nation's largest. The venue was the top floor, an open conference room with floor-to-ceiling windows all around offering a monumental view of New York City. The audience was the bank's top executive team and its HR department, about fifty people. The topic they'd asked me to address was the intersection between the bank's strategy, its leadership development program, and its HR department, or more accurately the lack of any intersection.

Earlier they'd briefed me on the problem the meeting was really called to address: the bank was recruiting talented women and minorities but promptly losing them once they experienced the organization's operating culture.

The formal session went fine, but things didn't get interesting for me until it was over.

That's when I went into a small kitchen off the meeting room to get a cup of coffee and leave the group to do what groups do after a session—compare notes, check for messages, exchange small talk. I'd just poured my coffee when the bank's president came into the kitchen looking for me. I was not happy to see him.

For one thing, I wasn't in the mood to have him critique my remarks, especially since it was his bank that wasn't walking its talk. For another, I didn't like his looks. He looked like he'd been sent by central casting to play the role of "bank president." Black patent leather hair with just the right amount of gray at the temples. Tall with a country-club athlete's swagger. A perfect blue suit, a perfect white shirt, a perfect rep tie. I took one look at him over my coffee cup and I thought I knew why the bank might be having problems retaining its best women and minority employees.

"I liked your talk," he said, shaking my hand. "But you didn't discuss recruiting strategies. I thought you might like to know what we're doing."

This was not what I'd expected to hear.

"We've found that everybody wants to recruit the same people," he said. "Everyone's going after the top 5 percent to 10 percent of the graduates from the same schools—from HBS, Wharton, Stanford, you know the schools. McKinsey, BCG, Goldman, everyone in consulting and banking, they all want the same people. It makes no sense."

This was really not what I'd expected to hear.

"This is what we're doing," he said. "We're sending people to Louisiana and Mississippi to no-name programs and no-status schools. The pedigree isn't as famous but the people at the top of their classes are just as good—and a lot hungrier. We're getting great talent without the usual baggage."

We chatted a little more, he thanked me again for coming, and then he headed back out to mingle with the people in the conference room.

I never got to thank him properly. Just for telling his team the few things I knew, I'd learned a big lesson from him.

So What?

We've gotten over credentialism in sports, the arts, even politics. In the world of business, for reasons that escape me, it's alive and well. Business school deans may deny it publicly, but privately they jealously examine the annual rankings to see where they stand. Applicants may act blasé about it as well, but they all know where their schools of choice rank. And recruiters from the blue chip firms make it a point to take the top prospects out to dinner and offer them healthy signing bonuses.

Talent matters. But credentials?

When he was dean of the Harvard Business School, John McArthur used to joke that he'd short any industry as soon as it hired a disproportionate number of HBS graduates. Warren Buffett recently told students that the things that go untaught at business schools are the things he values most: writing, speaking, and communication. When it comes to entrepreneurship, Guy Kawasaki, an original Apple evangelist, recently said, "I don't think an MBA matters very much for starting a company."

More and more the word is getting out: "Hire for attitude, train for skill." In a fast-changing economy, people will need to learn and adapt all the time. Credentials are no guarantee of an open mind and a passion for change. As the needs of their clients change, consulting firms are changing their hiring portfolios: people with backgrounds in sociology, anthropology, psychology, and other social sciences are just as valuable as MBAs. Recognizing that they need to develop their own people, companies have put more emphasis on their in-house universities. It's cheaper and more effective than hiring newly minted MBAs and then retraining them.

So if credentials matter less, what matters more?

Speaking to a group of prospective MBAs, Warren Buffett posed the following challenge: Suppose you could own 10 percent of the future earnings of any one of your classmates. Whose stock would you buy? Buffett then gave his answer to the question. You wouldn't pick the one with the highest IQ or best grades. Anyone in the class would be smart enough to be a good investment, and the differences wouldn't be enough to matter. Instead, he said, you'd pick the one with the personal qualities you most admired: the one who was most generous, most honest, who attracted others to want to work with him or her.

Then he reversed the thought experiment: If you were going to short someone's future, how would you make that pick? Again, it wouldn't be the one with the worst grades or poorest test results. We all know those aren't accurate predictors of future failure. Instead you'd short the person whose attributes were the most unattractive: an oversized ego, a lack of honesty, a disregard for ethics, or an unwillingness to be a team player.

Character, in other words.

Not the brand name on the diploma or titles on the resume.

It's not credentials that count. It's character.

That's the right way to bet on people and the right way to make your hires.

WHEN IT COMES TO BUSINESS,
IT HELPS IF YOU ACTUALLY KNOW
SOMETHING ABOUT SOMETHING.

When I arrived at the Harvard Business School everything I knew about business came from working in government.

That's not as ridiculous as it sounds. Working at the Department of Transportation, I'd had direct dealings with the CEOs of the Big Three automakers. I'd sat in on meetings with Eiji Toyoda and even with John DeLorean, who wanted government assistance to start his back-to-the-future car company. With rail, air, and trucking deregulation I'd learned something about industry economics. And earlier, in city government, I'd gotten a grassroots education in the kind of negotiations that went on to close a deal with a downtown developer.

That said, the first thing I learned at HBS was how much I had to learn. The professors I was working with not only were teaching at the school; many of them had graduated from the school. That meant they knew the library of case studies by heart. When I tried to read the cases they were like Teflon: nothing stuck. But after I'd been there a while, gone to faculty meetings, edited faculty pieces for *HBR*, and had lunch at the faculty dining hall, I started to get it, if only by osmosis. Business history, business policy, strategy, marketing, finance, human resources—I began to know the story and the backstory.

There was only one thing that bothered me: at the time HBS described its mission as the education of general managers. The idea was that if you read enough case studies and learned to recognize the patterns embedded in business, you could pretty much make a career of it in any industry. Somehow that seemed at odds with practical experience.

Take Apple. Steve Jobs recruited John Sculley from Pepsi to run the computer company. That made no sense to me. John Sculley knew fizzy water, not GUI computers. Lee Iacocca got credit for rescuing Chrysler—but did that make him a legitimate candidate for president? If you were a general manager, could you run anything, from a car company to the country, from a soda company to a computer company? Was there a universal general manager playbook that applied to every company and every situation?

Didn't you need subject matter expertise?

Then I left *HBR* and Bill Taylor and I started *Fast Company*. Bill had run the *Sloan Management Review* at MIT and then worked at *HBR*; I'd run *HBR*. We both actually knew a lot about business, management, and publishing. We both had deep Rolodexes of smart people we could turn to for advice when it came to the real work of creating a magazine and filling it with fresh ideas about the changing world of work. We had a lot to learn, but we had a lot to draw on—enough to get the magazine started and established.

And then came the dot-com boom. All of a sudden business magazines were the place to be. Advertisers clamored for pages to buy; venture capitalists sized up new publications to invest in. Where there are advertising dollars and investment dollars there will be new magazines. Think of magazines as Wonder bread and all those dollars as gravy.

I remember looking at the sudden explosion of hip business magazines with amazement. It wasn't that there were so many of them. It was that so many of them didn't know what they were talking about. It was if they were being run by general editors—the magazine equivalent of general managers. The sentences made sense; the design was the best part. But they didn't have a deep connection to business and the world of work. They knew what sounded cool but not what actually worked.

There wasn't any subject matter expertise.

Today when entrepreneurs show me their business plans I start with a version of my own Miranda warning: "I don't know anything about your industry, so take everything I say with a ton of salt." Because while I do respect the energy, creativity, and courage that goes into any start-up, I've learned that there's no substitute for knowing what you're talking about. Nothing beats knowing something about something.

So What?

If you read the popular business press these days you'll discover an implicit entrepreneurial business model in many of the profiles of successful start-ups.

· Begin by being between eighteen and twenty-five years old.

· Drop out of school. Or have a dormmate who's a nerd.

· Borrow money from family and friends or trick your classmates into paying extra for cups of beer at parties you and your nerdy roommate throw.

· Use the money to build a Web site for your idea.

· Watch your idea go viral.

· Sell it to Rupert Murdoch or a large media company trying to get hipper.

That's it. Think of it as flying without wings.

I have a slightly different model in mind.

It doesn't matter how old you are.

Start with something you feel passionate about. Don't think about getting rich. Think about something that you are driven to do. Something you would do even if it never made a dime.

Learn everything you can about your passion.

Read everything you can get your hands on. Find someone who knows more than you and glue yourself to them. Start a collection that displays your passion. Surround yourself with artifacts, history, examples, everything you can find about the thing you want to master.

Keep going until you know more than anyone about the one thing you care more about than anyone.

I'm not saying this is how to start a business. I'm definitely not saying this is how to get rich, famous, or even successful.

What I am saying is, this will take you places you want to go. It will make you a bona fide expert in the area you are most passionate about. It will set you apart from all those who have general information but no specific knowledge. And it will kick-start your ongoing exploration of the most important skill the future demands: the art of learning.

Not lifelong learning. Learning for life.

FAILURE ISN'T FAILING.
FAILURE IS FAILING TO TRY.

A re we going poor?" Amanda wanted to know.

My daughter was eleven at the time. The whole family was sitting around the kitchen table, but it was Amanda who had the most to say when I broke the news that I was leaving *HBR* to take a shot at starting my own magazine.

Amanda's question made a difficult conversation easier. I understood her anxiety: we'd moved from Portland to Boston so I could take a job at HBS. Adam had been four or five at the time; Amanda was just a newborn whose first bedroom was a closet big enough to hold her crib. They'd both grown up with me working at Harvard. Now that was about to end for something that didn't even exist.

But Amanda's question broke the tension.

Partly it was the way she asked it: "going poor." It sounds like "going bald" or "going blind," the kind of physical condition that kind of happens. It had never occurred to me that people could "go poor." The thought was good for a smile.

Partly it was that I could assure her that no, we weren't going to go poor. I'd put a safety net into place that would provide our family with income while Bill Taylor and I pursued our magazine dream. What I knew that Amanda didn't was that I'd actually be getting a raise the day I left *HBR*. That made it easy for me to tell her we'd be okay.

"You mean we won't have to sleep on the sidewalk?" she asked.

I promised her we wouldn't be sleeping outside.

What I couldn't explain at the time—and what she didn't ask—was why I was doing what I was doing. Why I had to do it, even if it meant failing.

The truth was I'd been thinking about leaving *HBR* for more than a year. The prospect of starting *Fast Company* only drove the decision—despite the fact that I was getting advice and pressure not to leave.

I'd told one senior faculty member I wasn't happy at *HBR*. Fine, he'd said. Stay at *HBR* but take it less seriously. Partner up with a faculty member to do some writing and research of my own. Use the *HBR* position as a platform for my own career.

Another urged me to stay on, but only for a year or two. Things had a way of sorting themselves out. If I stuck it out until then, the school would reward me for my service with an even better job.

More stature, more money, more security at an institution with unlimited prestige of its own—those were the arguments for staying. If I looked ten years into the future I could see myself still at HBS, maybe still at *HBR*. That was what made me decide to leave.

Fast Company had been stirring in my mind. It felt like

everything I'd done in my life up until then led to it, seamlessly, inevitably.

The question wasn't whether it was a good idea.

The question wasn't even whether it would work.

The question was, would I have the courage to try?

I was forty-five. I could stay at Harvard and do what my faculty friends were advising. But every year it would only get harder to leave. In five or ten years would I be able to take the leap into a risky magazine start-up?

I looked ten years into the future.

At age fifty-five, what would be the worst thing I could say about the decision I was facing at forty-five?

Was it that I'd tried to start a magazine and failed?

Or was it that I'd failed to try?

So What?

Let's pause for a moment and sing the praises of failure.

It's true, as Patton says at the beginning of the film *Patton*: Americans love a winner and will not tolerate a loser. But it's also true that the United States is one of the few countries in the world where you're allowed to fail and get a second chance, or as many chances as you need. You can't do that in Japan, or France, or Scandinavia, where conformity and homogeneity argue against risk taking. In those cultures anyone with the courage to flirt with failure risks permanent ostracism.

Silicon Valley is one of the few places in the world where venture capitalists go to work every day expecting a sizable percentage of their investments to fail. Not only that but they check the resumes of the entrepreneurs who send them business plans to see if they've failed in the past—not to punish them for failing but to reward them for it. The operating assumption is that if you haven't failed, you haven't stretched yourself far enough. Failure teaches lessons that can't be learned any other way.

At *Fast Company* we learned that the articles where the author was willing to talk about his failures were the ones that garnered the greatest reader response. Mort Meyerson's article "Everything I Thought I Knew About Leadership Is Wrong," in our second issue, helped put the magazine on the map. Here was a famous CEO who, with Ross Perot, had made EDS into a corporate powerhouse, telling the world about his failures as a leader. Articles in business magazines celebrate the larger-than-life virtues of CEOs. Or else they do a little muckraking to discover a leader's secret failings. But a CEO publicly confessing to his own shortcomings? Readers responded to Mort's honesty—and still do. To this day Mort gets e-mail from readers who find his piece for the first time and come away deeply touched by his reflections on business and life.

There's a lot to be said about the virtues of failure. But the most important thing about failure is that we need to think about it differently. To most businesspeople failure is like pain: you try to avoid it at all costs. It can hurt in so many ways—it can hurt your reputation, your bank account, your career. Failure or even the risk of failure can make cowards of us all.

What about you? How do you think about failure? Is it

something to be avoided at all costs? A painful punishment you want to escape from?

Turn it around the other way for a moment. Don't think about failure—or even success.

Think about what you aspire to. Do you want to make a difference? Have an impact with your work and your life? Leave some kind of imprint in business, in your community, with your family? What would you like to show for your time?

Answers to those questions don't come to those who play it safe. Those who play it safe aren't likely to ask those questions. And while playing it safe may appear to prevent failure, in reality it guarantees it.

"You can't ensure success," John Adams wrote his wife, Abigail. "You can only deserve it."

What he meant was, you can't fail as long as you're still trying.

If you weren't afraid of failing, what would you be trying today?

Ten years from now, what will you regret never having tried?

Every year for the past four years the Waldzell gathering has had some of the world's most inspiring men and women as speakers. And every year, regardless of who these famous people are or what they say, they are upstaged by an anonymous group of presenters: the Architects of the Future—young men and women chosen each year for the work they are doing to offer hope and help to the neediest people in the world.

They are not literally architects. Paulo Coelho gave them the name after he'd championed the idea of bringing together a group of young people from around the world as part of Waldzell. The thought was to give talented young social entrepreneurs a chance to learn from the world's thought leaders.

But here's the remarkable part: every year it's the Architects of the Future who do the teaching, the inspiring, and the uplifting. It doesn't matter who else is on the program. The people who come to Waldzell always leave talking about the work the Architects are doing. Although each one is given only five minutes to describe his or her project, the

Architects always get a standing ovation. It doesn't matter whether it's Richard Alderson, from the United Kingdom, who's training India's next generation of social entrepreneurs; Denisa Augustinova, from Slovakia, who's building a nonprofit to help at-risk children; Sari Bashi, from Israel, who's offering legal protection to 3.4 million Palestinian refugees; or Ridwan Gustiana, from Indonesia, who's providing emergency medical help in his country. The response is always the same: deep respect, admiration, and thankfulness that each is doing the work he or she has chosen.

Now here's the question: Why is it that when you have a chance to listen and talk to Frank Gehry, Isabel Allende, or Craig Venter, you end up moved and inspired by Nazrul Islam, Ola Shahba, and Ruth DeGolia?

The answer is that these young social entrepreneurs give us what we desperately need and want. They are pragmatic idealists. They are tough enough to wear their hearts on their sleeves. They bring us the rugged romanticism of young people who believe they can change the world and are willing to do the hard work to make it happen. That mix is what the world desperately needs, secretly wants—and will do everything in its power to disparage and discourage. What's inspirational about these young people—about tough and loving leaders everywhere—is that they are doing it anyway.

Most of the time when it comes to the pairing of toughness and love we get one or the other. Business magazines are filled with profiles of tough leaders who use their power in familiar ways: to make money, to build a career, to gain fame. Social causes are often championed by leaders who encourage us to show our love to the have-nots of the world:

to be generous, to reach out, to show compassion. The first tell us to accept the world as it is. The second tell us to wish the world could be different. Neither is much of a surprise.

What's different about leaders who are tough enough to wear their hearts on their sleeves is that they have a clear-eyed commitment to change that actually works. They are interested in more than good causes—they have to be real causes that stand a chance of winning. There is no honor in noble failure; radical pragmatism points to real results.

We're all tired of watching well-intentioned change agents sacrifice their lives in the name of doing good. We're tired of dying for our causes. We want to live for our causes—and see our causes succeed.

So What?

Jean Shinoda Bolen is an internationally acclaimed Jungian analyst and a professor of psychiatry at the University of California. Recently I heard her tell the story of Procrustes, taken from ancient Greek mythology. According to the story, Procrustes would set up his famous bed on the road to Athens. As a traveler approached, Procrustes would size him up: if he were tall, Procrustes would set the bed to be short; if he were short, he'd make it long. Each traveler would lie on Procrustes' bed. Parts that were too big for the bed were lopped off; parts that were too short were stretched. Every traveler left the bed altered to fit Procrustes' formula.

Today the Procrustean bed cuts and stretches business leaders and social activists to fit a modern mold. Tough-minded business leaders have their hearts removed before they can continue on their journey to Athens in search of success. Soft-hearted social activists have their toughness removed before they can set off to do their work of making change. Both end up badly served by Procrustes' bed.

The world is hungry for heart *and* for effectiveness. Not one at the expense of the other, but both together. That's what the Architects of the Future represent—inspiration and implementation. They make change through the current of inspired action.

Whether you're an aspiring social innovator or a corporate change agent, it's worthwhile to take a look at where you started and where you are now. Have you unknowingly submitted to Procrustes' bed?

When you started your work, what motivated you? Did you have a commitment to doing things differently? As you've made decisions along the way, how has your original intention changed? If you wanted to bring change to the world, no doubt the world has pushed back—that's how it works. Or if you sought to be a different kind of leader in a company, you've had resistance from within—no surprise there. But it's useful to take stock of the way you've reacted to the pushback. Have you gotten softer? Or harder? Have calluses covered over your heart? Or has a steady diet of defeat made you accept losing as your portion?

Now comes the hard part. Have you changed tactics—or have you compromised your values? Have you changed course—or have you abandoned your course?

The world is not an easy place for those who seek to change it. It doesn't welcome with a warm embrace those who say that the status quo is inadequate and who argue that just because things are the way they are now doesn't mean that's the way they're meant to be tomorrow.

That's okay; that's the Procrustean bed. Today there is another way to play the game. We're seeing the emergence of a new kind of leader in business, government, and nonprofits, people who combine radical hope with pragmatic solutions. These are leaders who aren't afraid that by wearing their heart on their sleeve they'll be derided as "weak" or "ineffective," because they've got serious practices and real results to demonstrate that tough leaders can have warm hearts. That's the kind of leadership the world needs. It's also what the world ultimately responds to.

EVERYONE'S AT THE CENTER OF THEIR MAP OF THE WORLD.

I was sitting on the Japan Airlines flight bound from Kennedy to Narita, about to start my Japan Society three-month fellowship. After months of schooling on all things Japan, I was finally on the plane carrying a set of three-ring binders crammed with company profiles and equipped with my official *meishi*.

Not that I was ready. It was a sixteen-hour flight, an endurance test. To comfort myself and see what I was in for, I pulled the Japan Airlines in-flight magazine out of the seat-back pocket. Maybe I could make the flight less daunting if I could trace the path between New York and Tokyo on the map.

That's when things got confusing.

I found the map of the world in the back of the magazine. I just couldn't find New York on the map of the world.

I do know where New York is. On a run-of-the-mill map of the United States, with Florida's finger poking down at the bottom right-hand corner, the hook of Texas in the middle, and California running up the left-hand side, New York is in the upper right-hand corner.

Not on this map. On this map California was on the right-hand side. San Francisco and Los Angeles were where New York was supposed to be.

I looked again. It stood to reason that if San Francisco and Los Angeles were where New York was supposed to be, New York would be where they usually were, on the left coast. I looked, and sure enough there it was.

Once I located New York the whole map started to make sense.

The problem wasn't that New York wasn't in the right place.

The problem was that the whole United States wasn't in the right place

This was a *Japan* Airlines map of the world, in which the United States wasn't at the center of the world. Japan was. A map of the world with Japan at the center meant the United States was upside down, which put New York on the left and San Francisco and Los Angeles on the right. My worldview put the United States at the center; every map I'd ever seen started from that point of view. The Japanese worldview put Japan in the center. Probably every map in Japan reflected that Japan-centric point of view.

I had to smile at my confusion and my new understanding: I hadn't even left New York yet and already I'd had my first lesson from my fellowship in Japan, a new way of making sense of the world.

As I sat there thinking about the difference between U.S. and Japanese maps of the world I had a second new understanding: it wasn't just the United States and Japan. Every nation saw itself at the center of the world and drew its maps accordingly.

Which was when it hit me: we're all simultaneously living at the center of the world.

So What?

Back in 1989 my Japan Airlines epiphany was mostly a metaphor and a much-needed lesson in geographic humility. Twenty years later it's a genuine fact of life.

Two decades ago some places were more at the center of the world than others. Wall Street was the world's financial center. Hollywood was the world's entertainment center. Milan was the world's fashion center. Madison Avenue was the world's advertising center. There was a place for everything, and everything was in its place.

Today if you want to check out the future of finance, you could go to Beijing—or to a Muslim country to learn about the rules that govern sharia finance. If you want to be a part of a world-class film industry, you could go to New Zealand, or to India to see how Bollywood works. The hottest advertising shops in the world? Try London, Tokyo, or San Francisco. Fashion? São Paulo, Berlin, or pretty much anyplace.

What's changed? Talent, technology, and power. Talented people no longer have to go to the old industry center to get their tickets punched. If you've got enough talent, you can work wherever you want. Other people with talent will find you, seek you out, and create a way to work with you.

That's where technology fits in. Once again, it's the enabler. As long as technology connects people wherever they choose to work and live, the center of your industry is pretty much wherever you are. Technology means we can comfortably work together without struggling to live together.

And then there's the issue of power. The old "keepers of the flame" who got to decide who mattered and who didn't no longer get to make that call. In industry after industry, "indie" describes where the most creative work is being done and where the most dynamic people are working.

These changes make three things true.

First, no place in the world is irrelevant. If you want to be a student of business and innovation, the whole world is your classroom.

Second, you can decide where you want to open up your own shop. You can make a calculated decision—China is the wave of the future, for instance—and do a stint in Beijing or Shenzhen as a part of your global education. Or you can decide that quality of life matters as much to you as raw economic drive and choose Colorado Springs or Asheville as your base of operations.

In Frank Sinatra's songbook, if you wanted to make it, you had to escape the little-town blues and head for New York, with the understanding that if you could make it there, you could make it anywhere. Now it's the other way around: you can make it anywhere—so why should you make it there?

Third, if you're a talented entrepreneur or aspiring professional and the choice of where to work and live is yours, what matters? What factors go into making your decision?

As always, the most important factor has to do with people. Are you in a place with enough smart, committed, high-energy people? Is the talent pool deep enough? Would more talented people come to work with you? What would it take to create a powerful draw?

The next thing that matters is technological infrastructure, including transportation. Can money and information flow without interruption? Can you, your customers, and your partners get to each other without excessive delays and hassles?

What about your community's IQ? Are there colleges and universities, think tanks, or training centers to raise the collective intelligence? If smarter wins—and it does—what is your community doing to attract, promote, and invest in brains?

How do you gauge the community energy level? More isn't necessarily better; hectic can be too much. But a community without a healthy buzz to it may be a hard place to start and staff a new enterprise.

What about the other values of the community? Is there civic engagement—do the people who live there care about the place they call home? Is there community empathy—do the people care about each other? Is there a feeling of future invention—do the people work toward a shared sense of what their community can be in the coming years?

It's a big world—and getting smaller all the time. It's not so much that the world is flat. It's that we're all connected. That Japan Airlines map had it right: you're in the middle, and so is everyone else.

IF YOU WANT TO MAKE CHANGE, START WITH AN ICONIC PROJECT.

In 1990 Rosanne Haggerty took a hard look at the way New York's social service agencies were dealing with the problem of chronic homelessness and decided she had to do something different. The officials and experts in charge of the problem appeared willing to tolerate the status quo; Rosanne was determined to end chronic homelessness. She had a model that combined the emotion of moral suasion with the practicality of economics. She had an organization, Common Ground, that she'd founded to undertake the mission. And she had a problem: how to move from plan to implementation. She had to demonstrate that her model would work while creating the conditions that would allow it to work. In other words, if change is a mathematical formula, she had to solve two equations at the same time.

The solution to her double dilemma presented itself in an unlikely guise. In the heart of Times Square stood the Times Square Hotel. At the time the area surrounding the hotel was squalid and dangerous; drug dealing, prostitution, and street crime had taken over. But if the surrounding neighborhood was dark, the Times Square Hotel was the heart of darkness. The deteriorating building was filled with people whose lives had already fallen apart. It provided a haven for the dealers, pimps, and prostitutes who plied their trade on the streets. When the building went up for sale, predictably no one wanted to buy it.

Except Rosanne. What she saw in the hotel from hell was an opportunity for an iconic project. She could use it to prove the validity of her model for change while simultaneously producing real change in the neighborhood and the lives of hundreds of homeless New Yorkers.

Since the first thing she needed was financial support to buy the building, she initially built her case around economics. And there was a compelling business case for the change she sought to create.

Did the city know that it cost up to three times as much to maintain a revolving door of services for the homeless as it would to provide housing? Did the city's major financial institutions realize that a cleaned-up Times Square Hotel could trigger an upgrade in the entire Times Square area? A successful hotel renovation—even one that substituted previously homeless men and women for drug dealers—could deliver an economic development boost for the whole neighborhood.

Before she was done Rosanne had won $41 million in support from the city and private backers such as Clorox and J. P. Morgan. The money would go to convert the Times Square Hotel from a haven for crack dealers to a working model of supportive housing for the city's chronically homeless.

First, Common Ground converted the squalid hotel into 652 small residential apartments with on-site social services for the previously homeless tenants. Then Rosanne went after brand-name businesses such as Ben & Jerry's and Starbucks to rent spaces in and near the building. Once again she was using a single stroke to solve two problems: the high-profile commercial partners provided jobs to the newly cleaned-up residents of the building, aiding in their recovery. And they reassured other businesses that the redevelopment of Times Square was for real. Before long Disney put an anchor store in the area, and Times Square was officially on its way back.

One iconic project demonstrated the viability of Rosanne's strategy to end homelessness and stimulated an ongoing renaissance for the whole neighborhood. It proved the counterintuitive point that a nonprofit could both save taxpayers' money and generate real profits for partners and investors. And it gave Rosanne a demonstration model for her larger strategy to end chronic homelessness, in New York and in other cities across America.

So What?

Change is the order of the day. Politicians promise it. Nonprofits design programs to produce it. Companies pay for training sessions to enable it.

The problem is, few people actually believe it. Change is too diffuse a concept to swallow whole. Change how? When? What?

The job of an iconic project is to make change believable. Once people can see it, feel it, and benefit from it, then change isn't an abstraction. It's real.

What can you learn about iconic projects from Rosanne Haggerty and the Times Square Hotel?

1. It's good to have a strategy. A model for how change will happen can guide your actions and provide a script you can use to convince others. Think of your model as a social action business plan. It needs as much discipline, rigor, and outside input as the tightest for-profit business plan. As you hone your plan you'll learn from others, identify targets of opportunity, and recruit allies whose help you'll need as you move from plan to reality.

2. For starters, focus on what's doable. Your first project has to work if you're going to generate credibility for your larger change strategy. Pick a project that represents your vision and stands a high chance of success. While you're developing your plan and filling in your strategy you're also scouting for the right project. At this point in your change effort every problem is also an opportunity. The biggest eyesore in Times Square was the perfect proving ground for Rosanne Haggerty's change effort.

3. The economics have to work. Remember the formula, "Change happens when the cost of the status quo is greater than the risk of change." If your project generates savings or produces new revenue, you immediately enhance your chances of success. You need the market to vote yes. When you make the economics work, you give the market another reason to vote for you.

4. Look for key partners. When Rosanne Haggerty added the city, Clorox, J. P. Morgan, Ben & Jerry's, and Starbucks to her team she got more than money. She got their endorsement, their clout, and their credibility. Even though their agendas overlapped only in part with hers, Rosanne was able to claim their full support.

5. Think of change like zoysia grass. A gardener creates a zoysia grass lawn by planting a plug. That establishes the basis for the lawn. Then you add a second plug. The two plugs start to grow toward each other. Over time an entire lawn emerges as the plugs cover the ground and gradually transform the landscape.

Your first iconic project is your first plug of zoysia grass. It establishes your credibility. It wins you converts. The first plug often suggests where the next should be planted. It begins to show others how your project can become a strategy. It may even generate new financial support, produce important political backing, and create new partnerships.

Most important, it makes the promise of change real. It transforms the audacity of hope into the audacity of results.

IF YOU WANT TO GROW AS A LEADER, YOU HAVE TO DISARM YOUR BORDER GUARDS.

The year was 1968. My brother Mark had completed his studies in Germany as a Fulbright scholar and I'd flown over to spend the summer with him touring Europe in the VW he'd bought. We went to Prague to enjoy the all-too-brief blossoming of the Prague Spring and then headed back to West Germany.

The only way back was through an East German corridor. We pulled up to a checkpoint, where heavily armed East German border guards controlled the traffic flow.

When it was our turn we handed over our passports to one of the guards, a big man in an East German army uniform with an automatic rifle slung over his shoulder. He took one look at our passports and waved us out of line over to a parking area. Then he disappeared into one of the guard booths that lined the border.

We sat in the parking area and watched the guards wave other cars through. After an hour we got tired of sitting in the car and got out to stretch. Another hour went by and we were still standing in the parking area. There was no sign of the guard who'd taken our passports. There was also no sign of our passports. We were in no-man's-land at an East German border checkpoint without our papers.

At the end of the third hour Mark had had enough. Sure, we were young and Americans and no doubt the East Germans thought it was fun to mess with us. What they didn't know was that Mark's German was so good he could pass for a native.

He got the attention of one of the guards. He wasn't the same one who'd marched off with our passports, but he and his gun were just as big and menacing. When the guard got close enough to hear, Mark said in perfect German, "One of your friends took our passports about three hours ago. He's probably over in West Berlin by now."

The guard turned on his heel and marched back to the booth. He came back with our passports and waved us to the front of the line, through the checkpoint, and across the border.

Here's the punch line: forty years later the border guards are gone, East Germany is no more, and the chancellor of a united Germany grew up in a country that no longer exists.

So What?

Whether we know it or not, we all employ border guards. Sometimes they're metaphorical; other times they're quite real. Either way the explanation is always the same: we need them for our own protection, for our survival. It almost always turns out the other way: the border guards become prison guards and what survives isn't what matters most. The higher you go in your career, the more successful you are in your work, the more guards you get and the higher the price you pay.

Take my experience at the Harvard Business School. When I first walked onto the campus it seemed like its own walled-off city. Even the layout of the grounds felt like a separate enclave surrounded by a moat. The gates were protected and only those who were invited could pass through.

After a while my initial reaction began to fade. It was great to be inside the gates. It meant I was one of the best and brightest. My *HBR* business card was like a passport, gaining me access to the faculty dining room, the library, the gym. My elite status was confirmed by the access I enjoyed to the inner sanctum.

When I left HBS, the gates came down with a crash. If I wanted to come back and visit a friend on the faculty, the border guards made me sign in, say whom I was visiting, and park in the area zoned for outsiders. It made me wonder: what did border guards keep out that HBS might want—or need—to let in? What was the price of this impenetrable defensive perimeter?

Of course it's not just countries and universities that close off their borders at their own expense. I've seen people do the same thing—usually leaders who do it as a way of protecting themselves from their own success. They start their careers as learners, open and accessible. As they move up the organization—usually because they were learners—they get overwhelmed by the demands and expectations others place on them. It's too much. They end up forming an invisible exoskeleton, protective shell-like body armor that surrounds them. It cuts down on the overwhelming pressure. But it comes at a price: the leader can't grow outside the border of the shell. Even worse, cut off from new energy, what's inside begins to shrivel and die. The leader who was a learner becomes just another tough guy. You see it in politicians, entrepreneurs, CEOs. They start out with a special spark. But when they shut down their own borders, the spark goes out. They end up with their own border guards—real and metaphorical—to control access to what's inside.

Is there anything you can do to keep yourself open, alive, accessible?

First, keep people around you who aren't afraid to speak truth to power. Leaders need people who will challenge and disagree with them. The system will routinely eliminate those people. Border guards in the form of administrative assistants or executive vice presidents keep these disagreeable people away from the boss. If you're the leader, whether you let them into your life—at home and at work—is a choice only you can make.

Second, remember to rub shoulders with real people. When George H. W. Bush was running for reelection as president, word got out he didn't know how much a gallon of milk cost. He went to a grocery store, the story went, and was surprised to see a scanner. True? Not true? Doesn't matter. The point is, people saw him as someone who didn't know what their ordinary lives were like. The way to defeat border guards is to make sure you go across borders. Grab brown-bag lunches at the community table. Take an unglitzy client to dinner. Answer your own phone—it works for Warren Buffett.

Third, don't ignore the emotional side of business. Back in 2002 Daniel Kahneman won the Nobel Prize in economics for his work on the emotional side of economics. Today we know business isn't all numbers and rationality. Emotional intelligence plays just as important a role in business success as raw IQ. Unfortunately, there's not much in business school or in business that educates leaders in the use of the right side of the brain. Few CEOs take time out to go to drawing class, take music lessons, or experiment with different forms of meditation.

Too bad. Because if you want your personal border guards to put down their guns, you may have to pick up a paintbrush. Or learn to speak fluent German.

ON THE WAY UP, PAY ATTENTION TO YOUR STRENGTHS; THEY'LL BE YOUR WEAKNESSES ON THE WAY DOWN.

John Doerr is widely considered the most influential venture capitalist of his generation. Which is why the book he once described to me when I was at *HBR* may be the most instructive business book never to be written.

"I've got all these old business plans in my desk," John said. He rattled off a list of amazing companies he'd backed at Kleiner Perkins, beginning with Compaq Computer. "In every case you can find the one sentence or paragraph that describes their unique business model advantage. It could be their unique distribution system or the retailing model. It's the factor that accounts for their success." Then John got to the interesting part. "It turns out that the factor that explains their success at the beginning is what accounts for their failure later."

I told John I didn't know how the world of venture capital worked—but I thought I knew a great book and a terrific *HBR* article when I heard it. It sounded like a cross between the best examples of HBS case studies and an experienced investor's thoughtful commentaries on how the ideas played out. Six to ten case studies would make a fascinating book in the art of entrepreneurship—with one chapter carved out as a contribution to *HBR*.

John never wrote the book, of course—or at least he hasn't yet.

But the idea stuck with me. There was a general principle that John had identified that made concrete sense. It was more than "What goes up must come down." It was that the very thing that took you up would be the same thing that brought you down. I began to see it as a universal law that could be applied to the rise and fall of companies, industries, even countries.

It explained how the U.S. auto industry's built-in advantages shifted to weaknesses when sudden market shifts favored well-built, fuel-efficient imports. It made sense out of the advantages U.S. newspapers depended on for decades, and how the Web turned those same advantages into vulnerabilities. Once you start applying John's principle to companies and industries, it turns into a paradigmatic parlor game. Today's losers, whether in media, airlines, retail, consumer products—you name it—first rode their distinctive idea to the top as an advantage, and then rode it back down to the bottom as a weakness.

And if it was true for companies, did it apply to countries? Could the competitive advantage of nations just as easily become the competitive disadvantage? What if fundamental market conditions such as energy, the environment, or global finance suddenly flipped? Would a whole national way of life turn into a national security danger if the global context changed?

So What?

Let's bring this rule back down from the global to the personal.

When it comes to your own performance at work, what's your greatest strength? And could it become your greatest vulnerability?

It happens in politics all the time; pollsters call it "semantic differential." It's basically Newton's third law applied to language: for every positive attribute, there's an equal and opposite negative attribute.

Let's say your greatest strength as a candidate is your intelligence and eloquence. Your opponent tries to convince voters to see you as an elitist who's all talk. On the other hand, if your greatest strength is your down-to-earth appeal to the common man, your opponent paints you as unschooled and unqualified in the sophisticated world of political leadership. As the old Chinese saying reminds us, "Every side always has another side."

What about your sides? Do you have the capacity to see yourself as others see you—say, your boss, a rival, or the people who work for you? If you were to write down on a three-by-five card your greatest strengths, could you flip it over and turn them into weaknesses? And what could you genuinely learn from the exercise?

Let's say your greatest personal asset is your smarts. It's a gift. You're a quick study, a fast synthesizer of ideas, a hard-wired idea machine.

Now think about the dark side of being that smart. Smug arrogance? An air of intellectual superiority? A lack of personal warmth?

For example, do you always insist on being the smartest person in the room? Are your ideas the only ones you promote? Do you ever compliment other people you work with for their ideas, or do you use your incredible brainpower to point out the flaws in their thinking and shoot down their ideas? How does the way you use your intelligence come across to the people who work with you? Are you intimidating to them? Or do they welcome the chance to be on a team with you?

Once you start to look at the gifts that got you where you are today, you can also see how they could hold you back from going any further—or even cause your downfall.

The point isn't that you need to renounce your strengths. Even if you developed new strengths, they'd have their own "other sides." The point is, once you see your assets from both sides, you can start to compensate for the dark side. All it takes is a little self-awareness to keep the force with you.

TAKE YOUR WORK SERIOUSLY.
YOURSELF, NOT SO MUCH.

It was the assignment of a lifetime: I was to moderate a dialog among four of the world's religious leaders. To my far left sat Ahmed Mohammed El-Tayyib, dean and rector of Al-Azhar University in Cairo. Next to him was Rabbi David Rosen, president of the International Jewish Committee for Interreligious Consultations and former chief rabbi of Ireland. To my far right sat Philip, Archbishop of Poltava and Kremenchug, a delegate to the conference sent by the patriarch of the Russian Orthodox Church. And directly to my right sat His Holiness the Dalai Lama.

My job was to lead them through a conversation touching on organized religion and spirituality, human conflict and business. At the end I had a specific question for each of them, a question I hoped would be polite but pointed.

Did Philip think his church and the Church of Rome would speak again within the next fifty years?

What could El-Tayyib say to reassure Westerners that the Koran did not condone terrorism?

Did Rabbi Rosen see Israel turning from a secular state to a religious one?

I reserved the last question for the Dalai Lama. It seemed fitting to end the session with his words.

"Given all that China is doing to Tibet—the railroad they've built, the crackdown on monks, the efforts to eradicate the language and traditions—do you think Buddhism can survive?"

I was seated at his elbow. Earlier in the session, to illustrate the painting on the ceiling of the Sistine Chapel, he'd held my arm and dramatically touched his forefinger to mine. Now I'd turned my chair so we were face-to-face.

He began his answer with the facts, without any sign of emotion. Here's how many Buddhists there were in the world. There were this many in Asia, this many in Europe, this many in North America. So, he said, it was clear. No matter what the Chinese did to Tibet, Buddhism was in no danger of disappearing from the world.

Then he turned to Tibet and China.

I'd expected him to be circumspect in his answer. The Chinese monitor everything he says. Even this trip had involved the usual Chinese efforts to keep him from meeting with heads of state and Tibetan supporters. My guess was he'd shy away from saying much about China.

I was wrong.

The problem with China and Tibet, the Dalai Lama began, wasn't the railroad they'd built or the large numbers of Chinese who were moving to Tibet. The real problem was they were the wrong Chinese. They were sending stupid Chinese to Tibet!

At this the whole audience was laughing. I couldn't help but grin at him.

The way the Chinese who were moving to Tibet cooked— their food was stupid. The way they interacted with the Tibetan people—clearly stupid. Everything would be much better for all concerned if the Chinese would just send smarter, better Chinese to Tibet instead of these stupid Chinese! He was clearly enjoying himself as he explored the various ways the Chinese who'd moved to Tibet were stupid.

Then he got to his last point.

We might not be aware of it, he said, but at that very moment there were a substantial number of Buddhists living in China. The number was large and growing. There was a deep spiritual hunger inside China and Buddhism was finding new practitioners who embraced its teachings.

With that going on inside China, the Dalai Lama said, who knew what might happen? Perhaps in the future the Buddhists would take over China!

He laughed that high-pitched full-body laugh that comes out of him with great ease and no warning. The people in the audience laughed with him, clapped for him, took great delight in his way of making sense and his sense of humor.

Later that night, I found myself reflecting on who he is and what he'd said. Here's an individual unique in all the world. His people look to him for spiritual guidance and political leadership; the world admires his message of compassion for all. A spiritual man, he delights in science; in answer to one of my questions he'd said that where science proves old Buddhist beliefs wrong, Buddhism needs to change. His country may disappear from the map of the world; he's busy studying the Jewish diaspora to learn how another people overcame its loss of a homeland. Every day when he's in Dharamsala,

India, the seat of his government in exile, he meets with Tibetans who've endured enormous hardships to flee their country.

And yet when I asked him a serious question about the prospects for his land and people, he gave an answer with at least two levels. His first response was factual, historical, and direct. His second response was playful, clever, and witty. It was a serious matter. And it was a laughing matter.

When I got home from the conference another thought struck me about his last comment, the one about Buddhism taking over China, the one that'd made us all laugh along with him. If you believe in reincarnation and you can take the long view of time and history, could he be right? Could Buddhism take root in China? Would spiritually hungry Chinese take to a philosophy that made them more Tibetan, rather than the Tibetans becoming more Chinese?

Which part of the Dalai Lama's answer was the serious part—and which part the joke?

So What?

Everyone I know takes their work seriously. You could be a woodworker, an aspiring entrepreneur, an architectural student, a professor of German. You could be working to be the best interior designer, landscape architect, contractor, cab driver, or coffee barista. Real people take their work seriously. What they do matters. It matters to them because it's a big part of who they are. It matters to their friends and families because they're depending on them. It matters to customers, clients, and colleagues because one way or another we're all in it together.

But what is it that separates people we want to work with from those we'd rather stay away from?

It isn't the importance of the work. It isn't the money. It isn't the chance to hang out with celebrities or claim a fancy job title.

The difference is in how people carry themselves. How they conduct themselves. How they come across to you. And how much time and space they make for you in their lives.

The way Ted Levitt ran *HBR* describes what I'm talking about. Ted took business seriously. He took ideas seriously. He took teaching at HBS seriously and he absolutely took *HBR* seriously. He only wanted to work with people who took that publication as much to heart as he did.

But his definition of the culture he wanted at *HBR* was pure Ted Levitt: "We should be like an Italian family," Ted said. "We fight like hell and then we go make love!"

We all want to work for people who take their work seriously—and themselves not so much. Who leave room for laughter. Who have time to tell stories. Who relish the mix of ideas that only an energized group can elicit. We want to work for people who are confident enough of who they are to be able to delight in making jokes at their own expense. Who bring others into the circle to make it larger, brighter, and a little lighter.

Work is hard. Life is short. Shouldn't we all rejoice at the seriousness of our work, and laugh at the foolishness that surrounds us?

STAY ALERT! THERE ARE TEACHERS EVERYWHERE.

I was sitting in an airplane flying over the middle of Europe listening to Hans Reitz tell his story. He was born in a tiny village in Bavaria, one of seven children. His mother ran a tavern; his father left when Hans was still a boy.

When he was seventeen or eighteen Hans saw the film *Gandhi*. Hans went to his mother and told her he had to go to India. With her blessing and next to no money he did what wanderers and seekers do: he found a teacher, he existed hand to mouth, he lived among the poor, he took it all in. He found the mystical and he found the miserable, and in the end, after years of study, he found what he'd been looking for.

Today Hans runs Europe's most creative corporate events company, counting the largest, most successful businesses among his clients. He also practices the spiritual lessons he learned in India, sprinkling small amounts of money into social enterprises. One of these projects is a coffee business with a Starbucks-like shop in the Frankfurt airport. Hans' employees dispense premium coffees made from beans that come from a coffee plantation in India. Hans pays the coffee farmer above-market prices for his beans and goes to the plantation as often as he can to learn.

On one of his trips Hans was talking with the farmer when he looked up and saw a band of monkeys eating the coffee beans off the plants. The monkeys were plundering the crop, costing the farmer real money. What should they do? Hans asked the farmer. Get a gun and shoot the monkeys?

The farmer told Hans, "If you start shooting monkeys, you'll spend the rest of your life shooting monkeys."

I took out a three-by-five card and wrote down the farmer's words. Hans became my teacher.

I was sitting across a long wooden table sharing a meal with Bill Liao, listening to his story. Bill Liao was born in Melbourne but now splits his time between Ireland and Switzerland. He describes himself as a forty-two-year-old serial entrepreneur who failed high school three times: the rote learning bored him stiff. By the time he was twelve he was building and programming computers. In 2003 Bill was deep into complex adaptive systems and social networking software and making contacts like crazy across the world of business. Bill and a friend were comparing notes when they discovered they shared a profound dislike for the way conventional social networking sites worked. There wasn't enough opportunity to build in the extended business relationships that defined networking in the real world of work. They decided to make something better: Xing.com.

Ninety days after Xing's founding the company was cash flow positive and has had positive quarters ever since. In 2006, Bill took Xing public in Frankfurt and the stock took off like a rocket. It became Germany's most successful technology IPO of 2006. Since then Bill's been acquiring other networks to add to his portfolio, and he's moved social entrepreneurship and philanthropy to the top of his personal agenda. His newest start-up: Neo.org, a social network designed, simply, to make the world a better place.

I asked Bill to tell me how he understood the value of social networks. How do they work? What makes them useful? What is their core value?

"Here's the thing," Bill said. He leaned across the narrow table. "Connectedness is effectiveness."

I pulled a three-by-five card out of my pocket and wrote it down. Bill became my teacher.

So What?

Hans and Bill and everybody else on Planet Earth are potential teachers—and we're all students of life.

You can't judge great teachers by their looks. Or their English. Or their profession. Or their education. Or where they were born, where they live, how they dress, how much money they make.

You simply have to stay open to what you're hearing and be willing to listen and learn. You may be with someone you've already written off when all of a sudden that person says something really smart, the kind of thing that makes you sit up like you just got hit between the eyes with a smart stick. It may even come out of your own mouth and leave you wondering, "Did I say that? I wonder where that came from. I wonder if I could do that again." You won't know if you're not listening.

You need to be alert. You need to pay attention. You need to be ready. Keep those three-by-five cards and a pen in your pocket, the way Ted Levitt did.

You want to be ready your whole life. Ready to learn, to listen, maybe even to teach.

It will make every day more valuable, for sure.

It will make your life more fulfilling as well.

And if you live long enough and learn well enough, it may even make you and me and all of us better people.

One last thought.

There aren't just fifty-two rules of thumb. And the most helpful ones aren't necessarily mine. They're yours and mine and all of ours combined.

We need these rules. We're living in unprecedented times. The economy changes daily, businesses morph constantly, old companies disappear in a flash, new ones are born instantaneously, politicians surprise us, new heroes emerge every day.

Change is the order of the day. The old rules don't seem to apply. Many of them don't work. Others don't seem to fit the new circumstances that confront us in our work and in our lives.

We're going to need some new rules of thumb. And as the game keeps changing we're going to need to keep renewing them.

No one knows them all. It doesn't work that way. We all know some. And we all do better when we share what we know.

Will you share your Rule #53?

You can add it to the conversation we're starting at www. rulesofthumbbook.com.

Reactions? Comments? Suggestions? E-mail alan@ rulesofthumbbook.com.

Tell us how you learned it, how you put it to use, what it means to you, and how you think we can make it work.

The best way to create the future we want is to share what we know with each other. You may have exactly the rule of thumb I need to hear. By sharing your rule you may inspire others to share theirs. We could end up with a whole new set of truths for this time, a code that fits the way we want to work and live now and in the years ahead.

That's the way it works.

You can think of it as a rule of thumb.

Rule #53

YOUR RULE
GOES HERE

Rules For the Road.

All 52 Rules of Thumb for you to clip and carry in case you need them on the road.

Rule #1: When the going gets tough, the tough relax.

Rule #2: Every company is running for office. To win, give the voters what they want.

Rule #3: Ask the last question first.

Rule #4: Don't implement solutions. Prevent problems.

Rule #5: Change is a math formula.

Rule #6: If you want to see with fresh eyes, reframe the picture.

Rule #7: The system is the solution.

Rule #8: New realities demand new categories.

Rule #9: Nothing happens until money changes hands.

Rule #10: A good question beats a good answer.

Rule #11: We've moved from an either/or past to a both/and future.

Rule #12: The difference between a crisis and an opportunity is when you learn about it.

Rule #13: Learn to take no as a question.

Rule #14: You don't know if you don't go.

Rule #15: Every start-up needs four things: change, connections, conversation, and community.

Rule #16: Facts are facts; stories are how we learn.

Rule #17: Entrepreneurs choose serendipity over efficiency.

Rule #18: Knowing it ain't the same as doing it.

Rule #19: Memo to leaders: focus on the signal-to-noise ratio.

Rule #20: Speed = strategy.

Rule #21: Great leaders answer Tom Peters' great question: "How can I capture the world's imagination?"

Rule #22: Learn to see the world through the eyes of your customer.

Rule #23: Keep two lists: What gets you up in the morning? What keeps you up at night?

Rule #24: If you want to change the game, change the economics of how the game is played.

Rule #25: If you want to change the game, change customer expectations.

Rule #26: The soft stuff is the hard stuff.

Rule #27: If you want to be like Google, learn Megan Smith's three rules.

Rule #28: Good design is table stakes. Great design wins.

Rule #29: Words matter.

Rule #30: The likeliest sources of great ideas are in the most unlikely places.

Rule #31: Everything communicates.

Rule #32: Content isn't king. Context is king.

Rule #33: Everything is a performance.

Rule #34: Simplicity is the new currency.

Rule #35: The Red Auerbach management principle: loyalty is a two-way street.

Rule #36: Message to entrepreneurs: managing your emotional flow is more critical than managing your cash flow.

Rule #37: All money is not created equal.

Rule #38: If you want to think big, start small.

Rule #39: "Serious fun" isn't an oxymoron; it's how you win.

Rule #40: Technology is about changing how we work.

Rule #41: If you want to be a real leader, first get real about leadership.

Rule #42: The survival of the fittest is the business case for diversity.

Rule #43: Don't confuse credentials with talent.

Rule #44: When it comes to business, it helps if you actually know something about something.

Rule #45: Failure isn't failing. Failure is failing to try.

Rule #46: Tough leaders wear their hearts on their sleeves.

Rule #47: Everyone's at the center of their map of the world.

Rule #48: If you want to make change, start with an iconic project.

Rule #49: If you want to grow as a leader, you have to disarm your border guards.

Rule #50: On the way up, pay attention to your strengths; they'll be your weaknesses on the way down.

Rule #51: Take your work seriously. Yourself, not so much.

Rule #52: Stay alert! There are teachers everywhere.

At the start of this project, before I'd written a single rule, I generated a list of all the people whom I hoped to be able to mention as teachers, mentors, and fellow travelers. If I'd used that list as an organizing principle for the book instead of rules—a kind of "meetings with remarkable businesspeople"—I would have had to produce a personal encyclopedia. There are simply too many people to whom I am justifiably grateful. Measuring my life by my friends makes me one of the wealthiest individuals in the world.

So for purposes of an appreciation, I'll have to be selective rather than all-inclusive. Rest assured that if you're not mentioned by name and you know you should be, when I see you I'll thank you in person.

Let's start with Richard S. Pine, agent extraordinaire, trusted counselor, advisor, friend, and unerring editorial guide. Without Richard there would be no *Rules of Thumb*; he not only named this project, he midwifed it.

At Collins, Hollis Heimbouch provided boundless enthusiasm, energy, and encouragement; her belief in this project was instrumental to its realization. Ben Steinberg consistently demonstrated his knowledge of the actual readership of this book and used his finely tuned ear for the words on the page to make spot-on suggestions to improve them.

How do you name and thank all the people who contributed to a book that took sixty years to write? A quick summary:

To my classmates at Amherst College and especially the team that put out the *Amherst Student*, a beta version of *Fast Company*—notably Richard Meeker and Robert Nathan, who forty years later continue to critique my writing and thinking to my benefit;

To Neil Goldschmidt and the whole team in Portland city government and the grassroots movement that made Portland what it is today—especially Ron Buel, Bill Scott, Bing and Carolyn Sheldon, Len Bergstein, Douglas Wright, Vera Katz—and the overachievers at *Willamette Week*, particularly Peter Sistrom, Susan Orlean, Phil Keisling, and Tony Bianco;

To the Harvard Business School folks who brought me there to work on a book on the auto industry, opening a whole new chapter in my life—Mal Salter, Davis Dyer, John McArthur—and the hardworking group at the *Harvard Business Review*, led by Ted Levitt and supported by great talents including Nan Stone, Bernie Avishai, Robert Howard, Tom Teal, Gerry Willigan, and more;

To the *Fast Company* superstars—beginning with Bill Taylor, Patrick Mitchell, Bill Breen, Linda Sepp, Polly La-Barre, Christina Novicki, Dawn Nadeau, Gina Imperato, Anna Muoio, and a masthead filled with the best friends anyone could ever want;

To my new friends at Waldzell and in Austria—Ernst and Andrea Scholdan, Thomas Plötzeneder, Andreas Salcher, and Gundula Schatz;

To the KaosPilots spread across Scandinavia, the Tanzanian "inventurers," the San Francisco creative partners, my Brookline soccer buddies, the Santa Fe coffee klatschers and Chaco Canyon explorers, the Japanese business innovators, and my São Paulo family of the heart;

I can only say many thanks for all you've shared with me and taught to me.

And to Frances, Adam, and Amanda: you know that rule about asking the last question first and knowing the point of the exercise? In case you didn't already know it, you are the answer to the question.